A BRIEF

HISTORY OF PHILOSOPHY

A. M. D. G.

A BRIEF

HISTORY OF PHILOSOPHY

BY

REV. CHARLES COPPENS, S.J.,

AUTHOR OF BRIEF TEXT-BOOKS ON LOGIC AND METAPHYSICS, ETHICS, ORATORY,
RHETORIC, THE SYSTEMATIC STUDY OF THE CATHOLIC RELIGION, AND
LECTURES ON MORAL PRINCIPLES AND MEDICAL PRACTICE.

NEW YORK

SCHWARTZ, KIRWIN & FAUSS

42 BARCLAY STREET

PREFACE.

Having composed and published brief text-books on Logic, Metaphysics and Ethics, which have obtained a considerable circulation in Colleges and Academies, the author of this little volume has frequently been urged to complete the series by adding an equally brief synopsis of the History of Philosophy. Many learned works on this subject are before the public; but they are mostly in foreign languages or written in a spirit alien, if not hostile, to Catholic thought. And yet, as the Catholic Church stands alone in its permanent strength and grandeur among the hundreds of religions in the world, so too its Philosophy is preëminent among the countless speculations of ancient and modern times.

There is, however, this difference, that the Church's infallibility in teaching religion is a supernatural endowment, given to it and maintained in it by its Divine Founder, Jesus Christ; whereas Catholic philosophers, like all others, derive their doctrines directly from human reason, but they are usually guarded from important errors by their knowledge of Revelation.

For more advanced students there exist in English two excellent works: Dr. Albert Stoeckl's "Handbook of the History of Philosophy," translated by Father T. A. Finlay, S. J., and Dr. William Turner's "History of Philosophy." But the translation of the former is still incomplete and neither of them is elementary enough for mere beginners. These will either leave the subject severely alone, as they now usually do, or they must struggle under excessive difficulties, unless a much eas-

iii

7950

ier and briefer text-book be provided, such as our summary is intended to be.

An elementary treatise like this may also be found useful and interesting for many persons of mature age who have never enjoyed the advantages of thorough studies, and who yet desire to acquire correct views on the ordinary speculations of the learned, or at least to know what leaders and what currents of thought they can securely follow, and of what dangers they should beware.

If the presentation of the subject in these pages is very elementary, as it is acknowledged to be, the uncommon brevity and simplicity aimed at are pleaded in excuse. This brevity has been especially studied in the earliest portions of the history, because the theories explained in them are so crude and obviously false that the knowledge of their fuller details seems to be of little profit to the youthful mind. In such matters to make a judicious selection of what should be presented and what omitted is as important as it is difficult.

There is still another useful purpose which this compendium may serve, namely as a collection of syllabi of such lectures on the History of Philosophy as are given to more advanced students in Colleges and Universities. For such intent a comprehensive brevity is a very desirable feature.

The Author.

St. Ignatius College, Chicago, Ill.

July 12, 1909.

TABLE OF CONTENTS.

INTRODUCTORY.

1. **The history of philosophy** is the history of the efforts made by the human mind to reach by discursive thought the deepest reasons of all things; that is, to understand their intimate nature, their first causes and their ultimate destinies.

We are not to suppose that men in the earliest ages were in total ignorance on these important matters. On the contrary, we find that many of the most remote traditions of the human race, as traced by students of antiquity among various nations, were much nobler and more conformable to the truth than some doctrines invented by philosophers in later times. But those primeval teachings were remnants of the original revelation made directly by the Creator to our first parents. As such they do not strictly belong to philosophy, because this science embraces only such knowledge as is attained by natural reason.

2. Yet it is important to note the existence of this **primitive teaching**; for it sets aside the modern scientific speculations of those who love to describe the first men as savages but little elevated above the brute beasts; as is done, for instance, by Dr. Blair, in his well-known lectures on rhetoric (Lect. VI). The facts of history are at variance with such theories. "It cannot be denied," writes Frederick von Schlegel in his " Esthetic and Miscellaneous Works" (p. 71), "that the early Indian pos-

sessed a knowledge of the true God. All their writings are replete with sentiments and expressions noble, clear and severely grand, as deeply conceived and as reverentially expressed as in any human language in which men have spoken of their God."

The possession of the highest truths by our early ancestors is more fully explained and proved by the Rev. Augustus J. Thebaud, S.J., in his learned work entitled "Gentilism—Religion Previous to Christianity"; for instance on pages 30–39, 290, 494, etc. On page 139 he quotes from William Jones's "Extracts from the Vedas" as follows: "Without hand or foot, He (God) runs rapidly and grasps firmly; without eyes He sees, without ears He hears all; He knows whatever can be known, and there is none who knows Him; Him the wise call the great, supreme, pervading Spirit."

3. The original tradition of revealed truth was in the course of ages gradually obscured and mixed with many errors, so that the remnants of it were no longer sufficient to satisfy the thoughtful mind. Then began various speculations on the nature and the origin of the world, giving rise to **philosophic systems.** The study of these is our task.

In almost all of them errors were blended with the truth. Now errors are not worth knowing for their own sake; but the study of errors enables us to understand the truth more distinctly, and aids us to appreciate it more highly, just as shading in a picture enhances by contrast the light and beauty of the more important features. Therefore, though the Scholastic system, taught in Catholic colleges and universities generally, presents the best answers that human reason has so far given to the great questions of the mind, still we derive from the study of other systems a clearer understanding of our own system, and we rest with increased satisfaction in the enjoyment of the treasure we therein possess.

Besides, this study is highly interesting, and it evokes a vigorous exercise of our mental powers. It is interesting, because it exhibits to our eyes nobler struggles than those of warriors, and more important discoveries than those made by travelers and explorers. It evokes a vigorous exercise of our mental powers, both in striving to understand many lofty and keen speculations of human thought, and in drawing the line of demarkation between what is true and what is false, what is certain and what is doubtful in their various systems.

4. The history of philosophy is obviously to be **divided into two periods**, the one antecedent and the other subsequent to the diffusion of the Christian revelation. For Christianity, when it arose, poured forth such a flood of light upon the great questions of the soul that philosophy in consequence underwent a vast transformation. The difference between these two divisions of philosophy is thus described by Dr. Albert Stoeckl in his "Handbook of the History of Philosophy," translated by Rev. T. A. Finlay, S. J.: "Christ is the central point of all history. His coming into the world has been called by the Apostle 'The fullness of time.' He was the scope and the consummation of the times that preceded Him; He was the point of departure for the time that followed; for the events that filled it have been hallowed by the redemption He effected. For the Christian all history is thus divided into two great periods; and, with the rest, the history of philosophy. This view is in strict accordance

with the facts of the case. The philosophy which preceded and that which followed Christ differ more widely
in character than the philosophies of any of the periods
subordinate to these. The world has never witnessed
such a revolution in human thought, such an enlarge-
ment of the range of human knowledge as that effected
by the introduction of Christianity," etc.

PART I.

PRE-CHRISTIAN PHILOSOPHY.

---

5. This part comprises **three portions,** regarding respectively: 1. The philosophy of the Eastern nations, 2. That of the Greeks, and 3. Roman and Alexandrian philosophy, down to the diffusion of Christianity.

SECTION I.

PHILOSOPHY OF THE EASTERN NATIONS.

CHAPTER I.

INDIA.

Two systems of philosophy obtained each a strong footing in India, *Brahmanism* and *Buddhism.* Both of them are intimately connected with the religions of their followers, from which they can scarcely be separated.

ARTICLE I. BRAHMANISM.

6. **Brahmanism** is the most ancient system of philosophy of which any record exists in the world's history. Its sacred writings are called *Vedas.* Some of its teachings are supposed to have been conceived 1600 years before Christ, though they may not have been committed to writing till about 400 B.C. Composed by different authors and at various times, they exhibit various philosophic speculations.

There are four Vedas, each containing two parts, prayers and doctrines. They are attributed to *Vyasa;* but, as this name means a compiler, it creates the presumption that they are the work of several authors. They teach sublime doctrines concerning God, the human soul, a future life, etc.; but mixed with these are gross errors of various kinds. The Brahmans worshiped a kind of Trinity called *Trimurti.* The first being, *Brahma,* buried first in deep sleep, was from eternity absorbed in self-contemplation.

3

7 9 50

His awaking from his slumbers gives existence to individual objects, which are said to *emanate* from him. Thus he becomes the *cause,* but not properly the *creator* of the world. For he does not produce the world out of nothing, but out of his own substance. As the sustaining power of things, he is called *Vishnu;* and the various incarnations of Vishnu are the subject of the sacred books. As the destroying power, he is styled *Siva* or *Shiva.* Everything returns again into Brahma, the absolute unity. The system is called the system of *Emanation.*

The *ethics* of Brahmanism teaches that it is the duty of man to strive after reunion with Brahma by sacrifice, penance and the contemplation of the supreme unity. Whatever soul fails to reach this perfection during life must migrate after death into some other body till it reaches that union. Those who had reached it were in later ages honored as gods. This doctrine of *Metempsychosis,* or migration of souls, is common to most Oriental nations, even to the present day.

In this system all the universe is only a modification of Brahma, just as the same substance is water at one time, then becomes vapor and then snow or ice; the system is one of real pantheism, everything being one substance with God. Yet some interpreters consider the emanations as really distinct from Brahma, as the web is distinct from the spider that spins it.

Article II.   Buddhism.

7. **Buddhism** is a still more pernicious error than the preceding. It arose much later; some say about the year 1000, others about 500 B.C. It seems to have originated in India. At the beginning of the Christian era it lay

like an incubus on Thibet, China, Ceylon, the whole Western peninsula of India, on Tartary and Northern Asia. It has remained in most of those regions to the present day, but modernized by agnosticism, and admitting national gods as incarnations of Buddha. (Cath. Missions, February, 1908.)

The author of that system is said to have been *Sakja-Muni*, the first Buddha. Schlegel calls it *pantheism*, because it admits no real being but God. Stoeckl styles it *nihilism*, and says: "Sakja-Muni, its author, has no God but nothingness. 'Nothingness,' so runs the first of the great truths of Buddhism, 'is the true being of all things'; all we take to be reality is void and without substance." Existence, or rather the clinging to individual existence, is the cause of all evil, the source of all suffering. It is therefore man's duty to shake himself free from this vain semblance of existence, or rather from his attachment to it. His end is to attain to the primary, the only true state of non-existence, to the extinction of his personal consciousness.

This annihilation is called *Nirvana*. It is attained by a course of frightful penances. By it the Buddhist becomes one with God, knowing the nothingness of all things. He can sin no more; like Sakja-Muni, he shares in the Divine honors which are due to Buddha. In such disciples as attain Nirvana the Deity is ever generated anew. Those who do not attain to Nirvana are condemned to wander over the earth in some spectral form.

The Buddhists became divided into several sects. Bloody wars between them and the Brahmans drove them to many lands. These errors of Indian philosophy appear all the more pitiful when they are contrasted with the contemporary sublime teachings of the Holy Bible. And yet some writers in Christian lands have striven of late years to invest the old errors of Asia with false attractive charms; as was done, for instance, by Edwin Arnold in his "Light of Asia." At the Congress of Religions of the Chicago World Exposition a similar purpose was fostered by some of the directors.

8. On the absurd and most pernicious system of Buddhism is founded the modern vagary of **Theosophy.** It claims to be a body of esoteric, or hidden, wisdom, revealed in the beginning of time, and contained in "the Book of All Truth." This book, as *Mme. Blavatsky* pretended when she inaugurated the imposture, and as *Mme. Besant* teaches to-day, is in the faithful custody of certain initiates, men of light and learning, dwelling in Thibet, and called *Mahatmas*, or great spirits, who by passing through severe ordeals and various metamorphoses, have developed their spiritual nature, and mastered all within them that is physical and passional. They understand the hidden wisdom, and by it can control the powers of nature, producing effects almost as marvelous as Christian miracles. Buddha, Confucius and even Christ Himself are classed among the Mahatmas. The ultimate reward is *Nirvana*, which, in this theory, is not annihilation, but absorption into the Divine reality.

Theosophy is an anti-Christian and godless system, using as its credentials imposture and real deviltry, as is proved by Rev. Richard Clarke, S.J., in his pamphlet styled "Theosophy." It is a modern form of ancient magic. That magic has real existence is clear from the Acts of the Apostles, Chapter VIII, and from various other passages of the Bible.

CHAPTER II.

PERSIA.

9. The religious teachings of the ancient Persians contained many elements of a philosophic character. Its main feature was **Dualism**, a belief in two first principles, *Ormuzd*, the source of all good, and *Ariman*, the source of all evil. Ormuzd is the infinite light, the supreme wisdom, the creator of the heavenly bodies, of the souls of men and of all that is good in the world. He was worshiped under the emblem of light or fire. In later times fire itself became the object of Persian adoration.

Ariman, who was good at first, envied Ormuzd and became evil. He created the *Daevas*, or evil spirits, darkness, winter, storms and all noxious plants and animals. At first the good spirit alone was worshiped; later the people strove to propitiate Ariman; and in order to do so they avoided good and promoted evil, making the whole country most miserable. They became even devil worshipers.

Then arose *Zarathushtra*, called in Greek *Zoroaster*, probably about the year 600 B.C. He restored the worship of Ormuzd, taught the Persians to till the fields, and opposed Ariman by the promotion of the arts and the destruction of noxious creatures. As an explanation of his religion, he wrote the sacred book called the *Zend Avesta*. In it he speaks of a mediating divinity, *Mithras*, an agent of good to mankind, who was expected ultimately to bring back Ariman to his original goodness.

7

The Persians had preserved many truths of the primitive revelation. For instance, their Avesta says: "I am wholly without doubt in the coming of the resurrection and the later body; in an invariable recompense of good deeds and their reward, and of bad deeds and their punishment, as well as in the continuance of Paradise." Their nice sense of right and wrong is shown in their form of confession, which partly runs thus: "That which was the wish of Ormuzd, the Creator, that which I ought to have done and have not done, what I ought to have spoken and have not spoken, what I ought to have thought and have not thought, of these sins I repent with thought, words and works, corporeal as well as spiritual, earthly as well as heavenly, and with the three words: Lord, I repent of my sin." The story of Ariman and his Daevas is evidently a perversion of the fall of the angels, who thenceforth made war on God, and caused themselves to be adored by the Gentiles; as David sings: "All the gods of the Gentiles are devils" (Ps. 95).

Dualism gained much favor with various Eastern nations; which was chiefly due to its popular explanation of evil, as proceeding from an evil first principle, and therefore not imputable to God. It was a leading error of the *Gnostics* in the first and second centuries of the Christian era, of the *Manicheans* in the third, and of the *Albigenses* in the twelfth century (n. 46). All these sectarians were not anti-Catholic only, but also anti-Christian. Still, because they opposed the Catholic Church, they usually enjoy the full sympathy of Protestants. (See *Points of History*, pages 60 to 66; also, for specimen extracts of the Zend Avesta, see the *Dublin Review* for July, 1906.)

CHAPTER III.

CHINA.

10. **The Chinese** showed but little power of philosophic speculation or abstract thought, but great tenacity in preserving received teachings. *Fohi* was the founder of their religious civilization, the inventor of their written language, and the author of the *Y-King*, which is the first of their sacred books.

The religious notions of the Chinese are as follows: the most excellent thing is Heaven; it is the object of Divine homage. Next comes the center of the earth, China, which maintains the balance and the harmony of the world. Man is the link that binds heaven and earth together; his duty is to preserve harmony. The fixed laws of harmony emanate from the center, that is from the sovereign, the father of the people. All the Chinese form one family divided into smaller groups; obedience to domestic law is every man's chief duty.

It is not known when Fohi lived; but about the year 500 B.C. there arose in China a renowned reformer, *Kun-fu-tse*, Confucius, who became the moral lawgiver and guide of his people for all future ages. His teachings were in conformity with the received traditions of the nation, chiefly inculcating self-restraint and moderation. Harmony, or concord, is the primary requirement of reason. This concord supposes that every man confines himself absolutely to his own place, within his own

9

sphere of action. Thus were the Chinese confirmed in the ultra-conservative traditions of their ancestors, which have kept the country in about the same condition for the last twenty-five centuries.

In all this there is conspicuous the absence of original and abstract thought. Whatever speculations have been found in China have been imported from abroad. Thus the sect of *Lao-tse*, whose doctrines are taught in a book called *Tao-te-king*, appears to be of Indian origin. It assumes the existence of a primary being, *Tao*, or Reason. The end which man must strive after is the rule of reason over passion. The sect of *Fo*, or *Foö*, is a low form of Buddhism: it teaches that all action is evil; absolute rest is perfection.

CHAPTER IV.

EGYPT AND WESTERN ASIA.

11. The early philosophic notions of the Egyptian races are wrapped in obscurity. The religions of Egypt and Western Asia were forms of **nature worship**. In Egypt *Osiris*, the Sun, was the active principle, producing all plastic energy in nature; the passive principle was the goddess *Isis*. In Western Asia, the former was called *Moloch* or *Baal*, the latter *Militta* or *Astarte*.

The nature worship of Egypt and Western Asia led to the grossest idolatry. The Egyptians adored the cat, the bull, the crocodile and even the plants of their gardens. In Greece the poets traced a genealogy of the gods which their countrymen worshiped, and which were chiefly these same powers of nature personified; the Romans adopted and enlarged the fiction.

Wherever the adoration of the powers of nature was introduced, at least in Egypt, Greece and Rome, secret rites were celebrated by those initiated in the **Mysteries,** as these meetings were called. In later times the grossest immoralities were practiced at those meetings, and the practices were continued till at least the fourth century of the Christian era. The Christian Fathers, in particular Clement of Alexandria toward the close of the second century, inveighed strongly against their immorality.

It is strange that this nature worship is exalted in the

esoteric doctrines of modern **Freemasonry** as the **" Light,"** the fuller knowledge of which is held up in the lower degrees as the precious great secret to be gradually revealed to the initiates in the higher degrees. The matter is fully explained in Albert Pike's *Morals and Dogmas of the Ancient and Accepted Scottish Rite of Freemasonry,* an analysis of which is found in the *American Ecclesiastical Review* for 1899 and 1900, entitled "Is Freemasonry Anti-Christian?"

Pike wrote this book for the instruction of the initiates, to whom he says: "The powers revealed in the Mysteries were all in reality nature gods" (p. 354); and (p. 231): "Though Masonry is identical with the ancient Mysteries, it is so only in this qualified sense that it presents but an imperfect image of their grandeur."

SECTION II.

GREEK PHILOSOPHY.

12. The Greeks were so prolific in philosophic speculations that there is scarcely a truth or an error in the
field of abstract thought which was not at some time or
other maintained by some of their writers. In their
eagerness for knowledge, they first sought for information in Egypt and Asia Minor; but they seem to have derived from those sources little more than a stimulus for
mental exertion. They began with the crudest guesses
at truth; but they did not stop till they had traced out
philosophic systems which have elicited the admiration
of all subsequent ages.

The first philosophers to gain the favor of the Greeks
were not abstract theorists, but practical men whose
pithy maxims, clearly and briefly enunciated, enlightened the mind and prompted the heart to prudent action
and to the cultivation of temperate habits. Seven of
these acquired such a reputation that they were called
the Seven Sages; namely *Solon,* the legislator of Athens,
Thales, the father of speculative philosophy, *Periander,*
Pittacus, Cleobulus, Chio and *Bias.* Here are some spec-
imens of their wise sayings: "Know thyself," "Avoid
excess," "Know thine opportunity," "Self-confidence
goes before a fall," " Be slow to resolve, swift to execute,"
"The greatest blessing is the power to do good," etc.

13. The philosophic systems taught successively by

various Greek speculators, and later on by Roman, belong to **three distinct periods :**

1. The Pre-Socratic period, which extended from 640 to 440 B.C. It was a period of preparation.

2. The period of Socrates, Plato and Aristotle, from 440 to 322 B.C.—the period of perfection.

3. The period of decay, from 322 B.C. to about 300 years after Christ.

CHAPTER I.

THE PERIOD OF PREPARATION.

14. In the seventh century before Christ the Grecian race did not occupy Greece alone, but also the sea coast of Asia Minor, many islands in the Mediterranean sea and several cities on the Italian peninsula. As they rose in power and wealth, they became more and more interested in the cultivation of various sciences, and in particular in philosophic speculations about the origin and the nature of the world around them. The theories thence resulting were of three chief varieties, the **Ionic**, the **Pythagorean** and the **Eleatic**.

Article I. The Ionic Philosophers.

The Ionians of Asia Minor appear to have been the first who attempted a solution of the problem which the universe presents to thoughtful minds. That the world was a vast mass of matter their senses testified; but it was everywhere full of motion and changes, and they asked themselves what was the first cause of all this activity. They supposed that the matter was all instinct with life, like one huge animal; whence their system is called **Hylozoism,** the theory of living matter (ὕλη, matter, ζωή, life). Their philosophers are usually distinguished into **two** classes, the **Earlier Ionians,** who were the first in the field of speculation, and the **Later Ionians,** who could profit by the labors of their predecessors.

15

The Earlier Ionians.

15. These did not speculate as to where the matter constituting the world came from, but what was the first principle of its multiform activity.

1. Thales, born at Miletus, 640 years before Christ, was the first to propound a theory on the subject. We have seen him numbered among the Seven Sages; he is said to have been so learned as to have, at that early day, predicted an eclipse of the Sun. He conjectured that *Water* was the first principle of action in the universe. Aristotle, who embodied in his Metaphysics a sort of history of philosophy, says about him: "Thales was perhaps led to this opinion by observing that the nutriment of all things is moist, that heat itself, by which living things are maintained in life, is educed from moisture . . . . and further that the seed from which living organisms spring is of its nature moist. But the principle making objects moist is water." Therefore Thales judged that water is the first principle of action in the universe.

2. Anaximander, born in the same city some thirty years later, thought that the first principle of action is the *boundless matter* itself, τὸ ἄπειρον, as he called it. He was the first among the Greeks to compose a treatise "On Nature," in which he teaches that a perpetual movement of revolution results in condensations of the world matter. In this way numberless worlds come into being—heavenly divinities—in the midst of which the earth, cylindrical in form, maintains itself at rest, owing to its being equally distant from all points of the heavenly sphere. Admitting, with Thales, that all living things come from moisture, or water, he supposes fishes to have been the first animals, which, when the earth became dry, changed their forms to those of land animals. The evolution theory is thus seen to be very ancient.

3. **Anaximenes,** some eighty years later, traced all energy in the world to the atmospheric *air;* he says: "As the soul within us, which is air (breath), holds our being together, so do the breath and air embrace the world." The life of the world was often spoken of by these philosophers as the "Deity."

The Later Ionians.

16. Among these, 1. **Heraclitus** (born 530 B.C.) maintained that an ethereal *fire* caused the world. Yet, as it produced an orderly world, it cannot have been blind, but must have been an intelligent force, a Fire-Spirit, which he called "Reason." Still he did not consider that spirit to be distinct from the matter, but only one of its qualities. This system, like all the preceding ones, is therefore monistic, not dualistic, as it would be called if the matter and the spirit were really distinct from each other. Yet it is an improvement on the former theories. Another leading feature of his teaching is that he considered all things as constantly changing, so that nothing "is" but everything is constantly "becoming." All things are flowing (πάντα ρεῖ), as he expressed it.

2. **Empedocles** supposes four elements: *earth, air, water* and *fire.* These are acted on by Love, which unites them, and by Hate, which drives them asunder. But all this movement is merely mechanical: no intelligence is working in it; it is a step backward. These four

elements continued to be admitted by philosophers, even
in the Middle Ages.

3. **Leusippus,** with his pupil **Democritus,** strays still
farther from the truth.   All things come from two principles: *Emptiness* or *Space,* and *Fullness,* by which word
he signifies countless atoms, or invisible particles moving
ceaselessly in space and uniting with one another to form
various bodies.   Thus all order results from mere chance,
as with the Darwinists of modern times.   The system,
called **Atomism,** was elaborated into much detail, so as
even to explain by it the working of sense perception,
which was said to be produced by atomic images striking
the eye, the ear, etc.

4. **Anaxagoras** (born about 500 B.C.) was of sounder
mind, and surpassed even Heraclitus in his approach to
the truth.   He made the reason, which controls the
primal matter, more truly spiritual, an intelligence distinct from matter, which he called *Mind* (νοῦς).   Matter itself he supposes to consist of homogeneous and
heterogeneous particles.   But he errs in making the
human soul, the brute soul, and the life of plants, parts
of that Divine mind.

Article II.   The Pythagoreans.

17. **Pythagoras** and his followers flourished, chiefly in
the Grecian colonies of Italy, about the same time as the
later Ionians.   Instead of speculating about the origin
of the world, they attempted to explain the essence of
things.   The system elaborated by them is very intricate
and ingenious, but not easily understood.   It is founded
on mathematics.   All things consist of **numbers :** both

souls and bodies are numbers or collections of numbers; by number and harmony the soul is bound to the body. God is the Divine monad, or unity, the basis of all number, the one cause of all corporeal entity, the ruler of the world. The soul is indestructible; after death it enters into a nobler or viler body according to its deserts. For *Metempsychosis* is one of Pythagoras's chief tenets. Ultimately, purified souls attain to incorporeal life, while degraded souls go down to Tartarus. The highest good on earth is virtue, which is harmony; it assimilates man to God.

Article III. The Eleatics.

18. The Eleatic philosophers were also contemporary with the later Ionians, most of them flourishing in the fifth century before Christ. The first of them was *Xenophanes*, of Clorophon, whose work was continued by his disciples *Parmenides* and *Zeno*, both of Elea, a city in Italy, and *Melissus*, of Samos. Their characteristic doctrine was that there existed **only one being,** rational, perfect, changeless, which they called God; all else is but a mass of deceptive appearances. Their chief arguments to prove this were as follows: 1. Nothing can begin to exist; for it could not have come from any cause unless it preëxisted in that cause. If it preëxisted, it did not begin to exist when it assumed its new form. Therefore nothing can begin to exist. 2. Nothing existing can move; for it would have to move into a vacuum, but a vacuum cannot exist because it has no being. 3. A moving body must pass through an infinite number of intermediate spaces before it can reach a certain place,

but the infinite cannot be passed; therefore the bodies
cannot get to any new place, they cannot move at all.
Yet our senses tell us that they move; therefore our
senses are deceptive. A doctrine so absurd could not
long deceive the keen-witted Greeks; but it paved the
way for the Sophists.

Article IV. The Sophists.

19. The Eleatic theory that bodies are only delusive
appearances, and the fallacies advanced to support it,
after a while discredited all speculation and led many
into scepticism, which was openly advocated by the
Sophists. This name, which means " wise men" was os-
tentatiously assumed by a class of cultured teachers, well
versed in literature, politics and the various other sciences, who, in the days of Athens' greatest power and
opulence, put themselves forward as the instructors of
the Grecian youths.

They pretended to carry the art of rhetoric to its highest perfection by teaching their pupils to speak glibly and
elegantly for or against any cause whatever, and to prove
the weaker argument to be the stronger. They undermined all virtue, setting aside religion, morality and
justice, and denying the existence of any certainty. All
truth was only relative, they maintained, true for such a
time and place, not for other times and places; nothing
was absolutely true and just. The Sophists made such
constant use of fallacious arguments that, since their time,
a fallacious argument has been called a *sophism.*

The chief Sophists were *Protagoras*, of Abdera, and
Gorgias, of Leontini. They taught in Athens and else-

where, about 430 B.C. Protagoras maintained the same error as the modern Agnostics. For instance, he wrote "Of the gods I can know nothing, neither that they are nor that they are not; there is much to prevent our attaining this knowledge—the obscurity of the subject and the shortness of life." Gorgias was more of a Nihilist than a Sceptic; for he entitled one of his works: "Nature, or the Non-Existing," a book full of sophisms, of course. For instance he reasons thus in it: the infinite cannot exist; for it would have to exist either in itself or in something else, but it can do neither. His teaching was the bankruptcy of all philosophy, and of all morality and religion.

CHAPTER II.

THE PERIOD OF PERFECTION.

20. The reaction of common sense against the sceptical theories of the Sophists was begun by *Socrates*, who unmasked their fallacies, and was continued by *Plato* and *Aristotle*, who built up systems of philosophy that have elicited the admiration of all subsequent ages. Plato is remarkable for his noble conceptions of God and the human soul and the relations between them; Aristotle for his keen analysis of the things knowable by reason, and for the systematic combination of all the elements of knowledge into a harmonious structure of philosophic science.

Athens was the battlefield on which the contest took place between these masterly leaders of thought and their various opponents. Up to their time speculation had dealt with the origin and the nature of the world; and only casual application had been made of various theories to the conduct of men. Socrates turned his chief attention to man's own nature and his moral duties: self-knowledge, theoretical and practical, was the direct object of his teaching. "Know thyself" he constantly inculcated; but this self-knowledge naturally led to the knowledge of God and of the future life.

ARTICLE I. SOCRATES.

21. **Socrates** was born in Athens, 471 B.C. He began by mastering the various systems of preceding philoso-

hers, which he found visionary, false and pernicious to
ind and morals. He felt himself prompted by what he
lled a Divine oracle to disabuse the youths of Athens
: all foolish speculations, and bring them to the plain
achings of common sense. He claimed that he often
eard the voice of a guardian spirit warning him and
irecting his conduct to this end. His professed purpose
as the inculcation of sound morality. In his arguments
e constantly insisted on the correct definition of terms
nd ideas. He would take up such statements as pre-
ented themselves in conversation or in the teaching of
le Sophists, and, by similes or oratorical inductions,
nd out the truths and the errors involved in them.
his peculiar method of teaching has been called *the So-
atic Method*. It consists in laying down no thesis, but
starting the mind a questioning about some familiar
ibject, thus gradually leading the hearers on, by what
styled *Socratic Irony*, to discover for themselves
eir own erroneous ideas or unproved assumptions, till
ley arrive at evident truth. Thus he disabused them
f false theories, and taught them the great truths that
lould regulate the life of man. See an example of this
eculiar process in Charles Bakewell's *Source Book in
hilosophy*, pp. 101–103.

Socrates is not known to have written any books; his
eachings have come down to us chiefly in a work of his
isciple Xenophon, entitled *Memorabilia Socratis*, and in
lato's dialogues. In these elegant compositions Plato pro-
esses to report various conversations of Socrates. These,
owever, are so much adorned and otherwise modified by
imself that the master exclaimed: "How many things
lat young man makes me say which I never uttered."

One serious error in the teaching of Socrates is that h⸱ considered virtue to be identical with knowledge, sayin⸱ that no man can knowingly do wrong, that ignorance i⸱ the one source of moral evil. This would do away wit⸱ free will and accountability.

Because his doctrines discredited the polytheism of th⸱ people, he was accused of corrupting the youth of Ath⸱ ens, and condemned to die by drinking hemlock. Pla⸱ to's dialogue called *Phaedo* narrates in a most elegan⸱ and touching manner the conversation held by Socrate⸱ with his disciples on the day of his unjust execution. It⸱ topic is the immortality of the soul.

Article II. Imperfect Followers of Socrates.

22. Socrates had several followers who founded ne⸱ systems of their own, departing widely from the wisdo⸱ of their master, usually by perverting or exaggeratin⸱ some of his teachings. The principal of these are th⸱ *Cynics* and the *Hedonists*.

I. **The Cynics.** The founder of these, named *Anti⸱ thenes*, took as his leading idea the principle that virt⸱ was not only the chief good of man, as Socrates ha⸱ taught, but that it was his only good, and that nothir⸱ else deserved any consideration whatever. His follo⸱ ers scoffed at honor, noble birth, riches, marriage, go⸱ ernment, and even at common decency; and from th⸱ snarling language, it would seem, and their brutal b⸱ havior they derived their appellation of Cynics, that i⸱ doglike (κυνικοί).

One of these disciples, *Diogenes*, is said to have live⸱ in a tub; and when Alexander the Great came to vis⸱

him, and asked what favor the philosopher might desire,
the latter, to show his self-sufficiency, simply asked the
monarch to stand aside and not obstruct the sunlight.

II. **The Hedonists, or Cyrenaics.** The founder of this
school was *Aristippus*, a native of Cyrene, who, like Socrates, made happiness the main purpose of life, but made
that happiness consist in the mere pleasure of the moment, and explained this pleasure as the sensation of
gentle emotion (ἡδονή), whence the name Hedonists.
In this system gentle pleasure of any kind is good and
worthy of man, and the principal object to be desired.
The more intense and the more lasting the pleasure the
better. Yet to enjoy such pleasure we need intelligence
and virtue. For *virtue* consists in self-control; and self-
control prevents us from indulging pleasure to injurious
excess and becoming its slaves; while *intelligence* must
show us the ways to procure pleasure, and to remove all
hindrances to its enjoyment. The Hedonists restricted
all knowledge to sensation, as if we were certain of nothing but our own feelings.

ARTICLE III.   PLATO.

23. **Plato,** born 428 B.C., was the most distinguished
of Socrates' disciples in social standing, natural gifts and
devotedness to philosophic studies. After his master's
death in 399, he traveled much in search of wisdom
through Greece, Egypt, Sicily and other lands. Having
returned to Athens, he lectured in the gardens of the
Academy, which for a hundred years remained the school
of his followers, whence they are called *Academicians*.
He published his teaching mostly in the form of elegant
dialogues; thirty-six of his treatises have been preserved.

7950

24. Plato elaborated a vast and consistent system of philosophy, of which the main doctrines are as follows:

1. *His peculiar theory of ideas* is a characteristic feature of his philosophy. Knowledge, he says correctly, supposes a mental grasp of the truth, that is, of objects; and scientific knowledge supposes a grasp of what is permanent and necessary in objects. For science is knowledge derived from universal causes, or general principles. By our senses we form *sensations* of individual things; which knowledge is contingent and variable. But we also have *concepts*, which represent the properties necessary and permanent in all the objects of a class, even in those individual objects of which we have had no sensations; for instance, the general concept of "a triangle," "a man," "an animal"; all of which concepts would still be the same even if no individual objects of them existed. They represent what is truly universal, unchangeable, independent of time and place.

These mental concepts Plato supposes to be derived from objective realities, which he calls *ideas*, which he imagined our soul must have perceived formerly in another state of existence, before it was banished from that ideal world and united to our bodies. In the present life, when I see, for instance, an animal, I recall the general idea "animal," which I beheld in my former state. But evidently this theory is only a guess, a mere myth; and knowledge based on a myth is unreliable.

2. *God.* That which is manifested by ideas is necessary; Plato confounds it with the supreme reality, or God. Ideas form the substance of His essence, or, as others interpret Plato's teaching, proceed from His es-

sence as plans come from the mind of an architect. God
forms various things on the model of these ideas, im-
pressing them on matter, which is an independent being
coeternal with Himself. But matter is not capable of
receiving the impression perfectly. Thus all imperfec-
tion, all evil, comes from matter and not from God.

3. *Cosmology.* God cannot have been created; and
He cannot have created matter, since its qualities are the
very opposite of His own: variable, multiple, passive, in-
definite. But God made the soul of the world. This
world-soul makes the matter active, but it cannot act
except in matter. By individualizing itself, it makes
the gods, the demons and human souls. These last were
formed in a higher and happier condition than they are
in now; but for some fault committed they were condemned to be united with their present bodies, on which
they act as a charioteer acts on his horses. In the material world are two principles: the *terrestrial*, without
which nothing is solid, and the *igneous*, without which
nothing is visible. But these two extremes could not
act on each other; therefore the world-soul made two intermediate elements, *air* and *water*, which bring the two
together. The world is like a living animal. Its motions in time constitute the *Great Periods.*

4. *Man.* The soul has *intelligence* and *love.* To its
ideas corresponds the love of the absolutely good; to its
sensations, sensual love. Between these higher and lower
parts are the supersensible passions of anger, ambition,
etc. The seat of ideas and of the highest love is in the
head, that of the higher passions in the heart, that of the
lower in the abdomen. We have three souls, the highest of which alone is intellectual.

5. *Logic* furnishes the rules which the intellect must follow in the investigation of truth.

6. *Morals* are the laws so regulating man's love and conduct as to make him imitate God. Now God acts according to His ideas; therefore man must do the same— he must make his higher love direct his passions. *The good* is the realization of the true; *the beautiful* is the splendor of truth; *moral good* consists in the harmony of the soul when all its parts are in a natural relation to one another; *vice* is discord in the soul. Plato teaches distinctly that man is free, but also that no one does wrong knowingly; two propositions which it is not easy to reconcile with each other.

7. *Politics* is the application of morality to social institutions, directing man to love what is truly good, and for this purpose removing all that divides men. Plato would even do away with marriage and private property, as fostering such divisions. He would admit only three social classes: namely, the thinkers, or rulers, corresponding to our ideas; the public force, corresponding to our higher passions; and the laborers, to the lower.

8. *The future life* will reward those who have acted according to their ideas, as God does, and punish those who have not. The soul after death enters into a new body suited to its virtues or vices, thus undergoing various metempsychoses till, at the end of ten thousand years, everything returns again to its primitive condition.

25. *The entire philosophy of Plato* exhibits a noble, powerful and poetic mind, grappling with the great problems of life and of the world around us with considerably more success than any of his predecessors, yet failing in several important points.

He strikingly displays before us the infinite greatness, goodness and wisdom of God, His unity and sovereignty over the world; the spirituality and immortality of the soul and the reward of virtue and punishment of vice. He also preserved some traditions of man's original innocence, his fall from grace and the existence of superior intelligences between God and man. But many of these teachings rest on no solid reasonings, and the many errors mixed with them show the limitations of a most highly gifted human mind.

ARTICLE IV. ARISTOTLE.

26. **Aristotle,** born at Stagira, 384 B.C., was for twenty years a pupil of Plato at Athens; later he was invited by Philip, King of Macedon, to come and educate his young son, Alexander the Great. Returning later to Athens he there opened a school in the gardens of the Lyceum, where he used to teach walking up and down with his disciples. From this practice arose their name of *Peripatetic* philosophers (περιπατέω, I walk about).

27. 1. His explanation of *human knowledge* rejects Plato's false theory of ideas. By a correct analysis of the processes of the human mind, Aristotle succeeded in giving a true and clear account of them, thus establishing our knowledge on a solid foundation. He teaches that from the *phantasms*, or brain images, resulting from our sensations, our mind forms *ideas* by its power of abstraction, considering separately various elements of the objects presented to the senses. His maxim is: " *Nihil est in intellectu quod prius non fuerat in sensu.*" " There is nothing in our intellect which was not first presented

to the senses." Thus our knowledge is evidently taken from the objective reality, and is therefore conformable to that reality; it is true. Our mind grasps notes or qualities which exist in every individual object of a class, say an animal; but it *abstracts*, or withdraws its consideration from all individualizing traits. The idea so formed is *universal*, realized in all the objects of a class, but the objects exist as individuals.

28. 2. His **Logic** distinguishes in objects their *genus, species, difference, properties* and *accidents;* and it explains such processes of reasoning as are taught in the text-books on Logic used in most Catholic colleges. Aristotle treats of judgments and propositions in his work entitled *De Interpretatione*, explaining their various kinds with their opposition and conversion. In his *Analytica Priora* he teaches the inductive and the deductive forms of reasoning, and explains some of the principal rules of the syllogism. In his *Analytica Posteriora* he establishes his theory of ideas, and points out the first truths from which all demonstration must begin, and which need not to be themselves demonstrated because the intellect (νοῦς) grasps them directly in their objective reality. His *Topica* deals with the Probable, or Dialectic, Syllogism; while his treatise *De Sophisticis Elenchis*, exposes the fallacies used by the Sophists.

3. In his **Physics** Aristotle considers the material universe with its workings or motions. He shows these to be ruled by universal laws, which work always for a purpose: " Nature does nothing in vain," " Nature is ever striving for the best." He recognizes in nature's workings a definite teleological concept, a plan of development; and therefore he admits the argument of design to

prove the existence of God; still he does not make this his principal proof of God's existence, as we shall see further on.

29. Having no idea of creation from nothing, he supposes matter to have existed from eternity; and, as *matter* must ever be some special kind of matter, *forms* must also have been from eternity. *Motion,* too, must have been without beginning, and therefore also *time,* which is nothing but the measure of succession in moving things. The *space* occupied by the world is actually finite, but potentially infinite.

The elements making up the world are those pointed out by Empedocles, namely *air, earth, water* and *fire;* to which Aristotle adds *ether,* which fills the celestial sphere above, and is the constituent of the heavenly bodies, *The earth* is in the center of the universe, spherical and stationary. Around it is the air, and beyond the air a sphere of fire. Surrounding all is "the First Heaven," that of the fixed stars, which is directly set in motion by the first mover, God. But how? Here Aristotle met with a great difficulty, which we shall explain further on.

30. *His theory of the constitution of bodies* is as follows: In every body there are two elements: the *primal matter,* which gives it extension; and the *form,* or quiddity, which gives it action of a certain kind, making it such or such matter, either iron or lead, a rose, a sparrow, a man, etc. The form is the principle of specification, the matter the principle of individuation.

Bodies rise above one another in perfection by a continual gradation. Lowest in the scale are the *inorganic,* or inanimate bodies; then follow *organic* bodies with merely vegetable life (plants); next come *brute animals;*

and lastly *man*, who is superior to all other material beings by his gift of reason, thereby sharing an attribute
of God. The form of an organic body, whether plant,
or animal or man, is called the *soul* (ψυχή); it is the life
principle, and the source of all the actions of the plant or
animal. The brute soul comprises the powers of the
vegetative as well as of the animal life; and the human
soul performs all the functions of vegetative, animal and
intellectual life. For in every body there is only one
principle of action, one form.

4. Aristotle's treatise on **Metaphysics** was so called
either because, among his works, it was put after the
Physics (μετά, after), or because it analyzes those realities which lie back of the physical properties of bodies;
for it deals with being as such, and investigates the ultimate principles or causes of all things. It corresponds
to what, in our philosophical text-books, is usually
denominated "General Metaphysics," or "Ontology."
Aristotle created this entire body of the deepest human
speculation, and at once brought it up to the highest
perfection it has ever reached, except as far as Divine
revelation has further illumined and extended its field of
thought. In this same treatise Aristotle also refutes the
philosophic theories of former teachers, thereby earning
for himself the title of "Father of the History of Philosophy."

31. 5. **Theology.** Aristotle proves the existence of
God as follows: Every being is either actual or potential.
The potential cannot become actual unless some other
being acts on it. If that second being is started into action by a third, that third must be actual. Thus we
must come to an ultimate active being which is not itself

acted upon, a first cause not caused, a first mover not moved by another. This being we call *God*. The only escape from this reasoning would be to suppose that there has been an infinite series of causes; but an infinite series could never have been gone through so as to reach a definite cause.

As to God's attributes Aristotle teaches, as corollaries from the nature of the First Cause, that God is: 1. *Absolutely simple*, excluding all parts; pure form without matter; all actuality, and one without a compeer. 2. While in man *knowledge* is an accident added to the substance, God's knowledge is Himself, not some accident added to him. Being self-sufficient, and finding perfect happiness in Himself, God could not, Aristotle thought, *will* anything out of Himself. Hence His activity is one of mere self-contemplation. Nor can He know anything outside Himself, because the thing known perfects the knower, and God cannot acquire any perfection from any other being.

32. Hence came the difficulty to which we referred above. If God could not know nor will anything outside of Himself, *how then can He move the world?* Aristotle answers this by saying that God is to the world an object of tendency or desire; for, being the supreme good, He is the object of tendency for all things, so that they are all drawn to Him. And as He is elevated above the world, all things move upward toward Him, every being doing so after its own nature. So likewise, since God cannot know anything out of Himself, he cannot exercise His providence over men or other things; yet all is well regulated by the general motion which He necessarily communicates to the whole world.

The fact that so powerful a mind as Aristotle's went so far astray in his speculations about God makes it strikingly evident that the teachings of the Old Testament could not have proceeded from merely human wisdom, much less could the doctrines of Christianity.

33. 6. **The Psychology** of Aristotle is far superior to his Theology. It is so perfect a production of his analytic mind that subsequent ages have not been able to improve upon its main features nor upon most of its details. In fact, to exhibit the discoveries which he made in this department of philosophy it would be necessary to explain nearly the entire treatise on Psychology as it is taught to-day in Catholic colleges. We must, however, point out some important *exceptions.*

(a) While Aristotle saw clearly enough that an intellectual soul cannot be evolved from matter, and therefore cannot proceed by mere generation from the parents, as does the life principle of plant and brute; while he stated even explicitly that it must come to man from without (θύραθεν), and therefore he calls it something Divine (θεῖον), he could not, on his theory that God does not act in the world, admit the truth that the human soul comes directly from God by creation. Yet Moses had written, eleven centuries before, in the second chapter of Genesis: "The Lord formed man out of the slime of the earth, and breathed into his face the breath of life, and he became a living soul." That there is an exigency in the nature of an intellectual being for some such origin Aristotle understood, but the manner of its accomplishment he failed to know.

(b) Similarly he nowhere speaks of the immortality of individual human souls. On this point, as on some others of great moment, he falls far behind Plato, who was therefore preferred to him by the early Christian writers.

34. 7. **The Ethics** of Aristotle suffers from some most serious defects. In particular, he does not rest our moral duties on their true foundation, the supreme dominion of God over His creatures. He also mistakes the nature of the supreme happiness to which all the conduct of man is to be directed. For, ignoring the immortality of the soul, Aristotle makes us look for beatitude in the present life. Yet he explains correctly that the true happiness of man must consist in virtue, which will bring him an enjoyment worthy of man's dignity.

35. 8. Under the head of Ethics we may consider the **Political Philosophy** of the author. It is superior to Plato's in not pushing State absolutism to the length of Socialism; but it is inferior to the latter's in providing for the enforcement of the laws no higher sanction than happiness or unhappiness in the present life. Aristotle rightly maintains the priority of the family to the State; and he therefore makes it the duty of the State to keep the family intact; but, at the same time, he errs grossly in requiring that, for the public good, children of imperfect bodily formation shall be destroyed, and the number of children shall be limited by law. He errs likewise in teaching that nature intends some men of less mental capacity to be slaves, and in refusing them all rights against their masters. He grants that to treat them cruelly is wrong; but he maintains that a cruel master does not violate their rights.

CHAPTER III.

THE PERIOD OF DECAY.

36. The battle of Chaeronea, which occurred in the year 338 B.C., put an end to the civil liberty of the Greeks, and with it to the golden age of their literature and philosophy. Then arose various novel theories, which continued for many centuries to exercise considerable influence among the learned men of Greece and Rome. The principal of these were three: *Stoicism, Epicureanism* and *Scepticism*.

ARTICLE I. STOICISM.

37. **Stoicism** is so called from the fact that its originator, *Zeno*, delivered his lectures in a porch (στοά). Born in Cyprus, and first engaged in commercial pursuits, he later betook himself to Athens, where, after attending the lectures of various teachers, at the age of sixty he set himself up as a master, and continued his work till, in the year 262 B.C., he died at the age of ninety-eight years.

In Logic he taught sensism, in Physics a mixture of materialism, pantheism and fatalism; but in all these branches of speculation he has left us nothing worthy of our attention. His *Ethics* deserves our study, not so much for its intrinsic worth, as for the great influence it exerted both over the Greeks and over the renowned men of Rome's classic age. It mainly treated the question: "How can an individual man obtain perfect happiness for himself in this world?" For, after the example of Aristotle, the Stoics lost sight of a future life.

Their answer to this question was, "by living conformably to nature," meaning by "nature" the law of the universal, or Divine, reason. Hence living according to nature meant leading a rational, or virtuous, life. Virtue, in this theory, is not to be sought on account of the enjoyment or pleasure it gives, but for its own sake: it is man's last end, his *summum bonum.* Virtue is called *the Right,* or *Proper;* it is not only man's greatest good, but his only good; all other things are indifferent.

The system taught also that virtue is essentially *one* and indivisible, so that the person who had one virtue had all the virtues, and whoever had one vice had all the vices. Even he who would closely approximate a life according to nature but fall below the mark in some respect was a vicious, wicked man. Another error of the Stoics was that no act is good or bad in itself, but any act becomes good or bad when it is done for a good or bad end. Again, they maintained that every bad man sins in every action, while every good man does right in every action.

They considered *the emotions,* or passions, as departures from the law of reason, and therefore as morally evil: the virtuous man yields to no emotion; he may feel pleasure or pain, but he is not influenced in his conduct by either. In this apathy (ἀπαθής, without feeling) consists the ideal perfection of the true sage. Such a sage is equal in happiness to Jove himself, except only in immortality. Whoever is not a sage is a fool; he is swayed by every passion. Excessive pride was the nat-

ural result for such as considered themselves among the
true members of the school.   Later Stoics, however, admitted various degrees of virtue, and granted that no one
could attain ideal virtue.

Article II.   Epicurean Philosophy.

38. The system of **Epicurus** dealt with the same question as the preceding, that of perfect happiness; but it
gave an answer diametrically opposed to the former.   It
claimed that the *summum bonum* is self-gratification,
while pain is the supreme evil of mankind.   In this leading tenet Epicurus, who was born 341 B.C., agreed with
the Hedonists (n. 22); but he modified that theory inasmuch as he exalted *painlessness*, or a state of permanent
enjoyment, above a succession of pleasures.

How is this painlessness acquired?   Epicurus answers:
"Pain is the disagreeable feeling experienced under the
pressure of some need or some desire.   Pain is absent
either when we can satisfy all our needs and desires, or
when we have neither needs nor desires which call for
satisfaction.   We can therefore attain to happiness in
two ways: either by supplying all our needs and satisfy-
ing all our desires, or by restricting our needs and desires to that measure which it is in our power to satisfy.
The first means is not possible to men—there is nothing
left for them but to restrict their needs."

To attain this purpose the following *rules* were laid
down: 1. Practice due moderation.   2. Avoid pleasures
which bring with them more pain than enjoyment.   3.
Admit pain which produces more pleasure than suffering.
In this balancing of pleasures against pains the Epicur-

eans admitted that spiritual pleasures can be greater than sensuous, if they react more pleasurably on the body; as, for instance, pleasant memories often do.

Hence *the great rule* of Epicurus is: "Calculate so that you may derive from your life the greatest possible amount of pleasure and the smallest possible amount of pain." This requires frugality, simple habits, friendship and abstinence from excess. Pleasure is the end, virtue the means to that end.

It is evident that this philosophic system destroys all true morality and even all honor. It was supported by a logic of sensism, and a physical theory resembling that of Democritus (n. 16-3), who considered the world as a conglomeration of material particles combined by mere chance; whence it would follow that man is in no way dependent on God. While the Stoic believed in fatalism, the Epicurean believed in casualism. This theory was extensively reduced to practice, and was for ages the strongest rival of the Stoic philosophy.

ARTICLE III.   SCEPTICISM.

39. *Pyrrho*, the father of **Scepticism,** was a contemporary of Aristotle. Like the Stoics and the Epicureans, he directed his philosophy to the attaining of happiness. He made this consist in *imperturbability.* Quiet of mind, he thought, was disturbed by deep research, which should therefore be avoided, especially since, after all, research is unprofitable. For in themselves things are neither beautiful nor hateful, neither great nor small, good nor bad, but all are indifferent: nothing is superior to anything

else. It becomes the wise man to preserve in every event complete tranquillity of mind. A similar philosophy is often heard in our own day, couched in the maxim: "it will be all the same in a hundred years from now." Though often uttered in mere jest, this saying constitutes for some persons the philosophy of their lives. The maxim is untrue: if we bear evils well, this will make us happier hereafter.

The Scepticism of Pyrrho differed from that of the Sophists (n. 19), because it did not merely trifle with certainty, like theirs, but it soberly maintained the uselessness of all study, and therefore it implied the death of all philosophy. Still practically some of its promoters studied hard, in order to defend their system by fallacious reasonings; in particular *Ænesidemus* laid down ten reasons in favor of universal doubt, vigorously attacking, among other principles, that of causality. (See Finlay's translation of Stoeckl's *History of Philosophy*, page 155.)

Article IV. Eclecticism.

40. When Pyrrho's Scepticism had discouraged all philosophic inquiry after certainty, an attempt was made to find a common speculative basis on which to erect a system of moral conduct. This basis was to be a working hypothesis resting on the common convictions of men. To this **Eclecticism** most followers of the other schools strove to adapt their systems. In various forms this kind of philosophy prevailed from about 150 B.C. till the rise of Christian philosophy.

No Greek philosophers of great name assumed the

leadership of the Eclectic school. In fact we can scarcely denominate it a "school"; it was merely a common tendency of writers belonging to various schools who put forward what appeared to be most plausible and practical in their several systems, thus trying to gain favor for their respective theories.

SECTION III.

PHILOSOPHY OF ROME AND ALEXANDRIA.

CHAPTER I.

PHILOSOPHY OF ROME.

41. Greek philosophic thought was long despised at Rome. As late as 161 B.C. a decree of the senate forbade philosophers and rhetoricians to dwell in the City. But after the conquest of Greece had established closer contact with its people, the more practical points of its philosophical systems began to be appreciated by the conquerors, many of whom became indoctrinated with the views of the Stoics, the Epicureans, the Sceptics and the Eclectics. The following are **the principal Roman philosophers.**

1. *Cicero* (106–43 B.C.) was an Eclectic philosopher. He was so far a sceptic that he despaired of arriving at perfect certainty; and he took probability for his guide of conduct. He accepted inborn judgments as trustworthy, and attributed to them the common sense of men. He proved the existence of God both by the argument of common consent and by that of design; namely, from the admirable providence manifested in the universe, which is evidently formed by a God of infinite wisdom.

The soul of man he considered as of heavenly origin. *In Ethics* he is a moderate Stoic, but he strongly opposes fatalism and defends human liberty. That is morally good, he maintains, which is intrinsically praiseworthy; virtue is the highest but not the only good of man, since honors, wealth, health, etc., contribute to a man's complete happiness.

It was especially during the last three years of his life that Cicero found his consolation in philosophy, which he labored earnestly to introduce among the Romans; and in this effort his success was considerable.

2. *Varro* (116–21 B.C.), who was called by Seneca the most learned of the Romans, was a Stoic and Eclectic.

3. *Lucretius* (95–51 B.C.) explained the doctrine of Epicurus in his classical poem *De Rerum Natura*, "On the Nature of Things."

4. *Seneca*, born in Cordova, Spain, was the teacher of Nero, by whose order he committed suicide in the year 65 after Christ. He was a thorough-going Stoic. He considered philosophy as the science of good and evil: "That is good which is conformable to reason; the wise man does not fear death, he even desires it when reason approves," etc. Such are his leading doctrines in ethics. In metaphysics he admits two first principles, God and matter; God is a spirit, and the souls of men are parts of God.

5. *Epictetus*, first a slave, then a freedman, wrote about the years 90 to 100 after Christ, laying his chief stress on the maxim "*sustine, abstine*," "bear and abstain," as far as this makes you independent of external things. Like most other original thinkers, he got hold of one leading idea, and made all other thoughts square with it.

6. *Marcus Aurelius*, who was Emperor of Rome from

A.D. 161 to 180, though a Stoic, expresses several sentiments worthy of a Christian, and which he may have borrowed from the Christians; for by that time Christianity had begun to illuminate the civilized portions of the earth. He wrote, for instance: "Let a man consider himself as a part of the whole, which is presided over by a wise and loving Father, to whose will he must submit." Hence followed resignation to the dispositions of Providence and kindness to all men. Even Seneca in his day had already caught some of the Christian spirit. Of late years efforts have been made by opponents of Christianity to circulate the writings of these two philosophers as rivaling the sublime doctrines of the Blessed Saviour.

CHAPTER II.

THE ALEXANDRIAN SCHOOLS.

42. Alexander the Great had founded the city of **Alexandria** in Egypt 332 years B.C.; and, mindful of his former master Aristotle, he had wished to make that city a new center of philosophic thought. His successors, the Ptolemies, inherited his spirit of admiration for literature and the fine arts; and under their influence Alexandria became a new Athens. Its *Museum* was a palace of learned scholars, while its library gathered rich treasures of Grecian, Roman, Jewish, Persian, Babylonian, Phœnician and Indian literature.

ARTICLE I. THE GRÆCO-JEWISH SCHOOLS.

43. **The Holy Scriptures** were translated into Greek at Alexandria, probably about 250 B.C.; the work is called the *Septuagint* version. Greek philosophers welcomed this treasury of new thoughts, both as affording matter for fresh speculations, and as suggesting a new basis for morality, which Scepticism had undermined. In the philosophy thence resulting it was natural that the religious element should predominate. The Jews strove to prove by elaborate efforts that all the best elements of Grecian philosophy had been derived from Holy Writ, in which they claimed the truth was wrapped in metaphor. Hence arose their method of explaining many portions

of the Scriptures as if they were only allegories; for some of the Jewish interpreters were little better than rationalists.

44. 1. *Philo the Jew*, as he is usually styled, who wrote about A.D. 50, was the most conspicuous and the ablest of the Jewish philosophers, and the leader of this school. He traced in the Holy Scriptures the teachings of Plato, Aristotle, Zeno and other ancient philosophers; but he did not succeed in blending those various elements into one harmonious whole.

For instance, Philo identifies Plato's ideas and ideal world, Plato's *Logos*, with the Divine Wisdom spoken of in the Sapiential Books; and he considers the visible world as an impression of that *Word* on matter, as a stamp is impressed on wax. He speaks of God as a most pure light, which is not knowable but by direct vision. The human soul is the effulgence of that light. It contains two parts: its rational part is composed of reason and speech, and the perfection of these is wisdom. Its irrational part consists of passions and desires, whose perfection lies in courage and moderation. Good souls are rewarded after death; evil souls must migrate into other bodies.

45. 2. **The Talmudists** made a still more arbitrary mixture of Jewish and Greek philosophy. Their *Mishnah*, written in the second century after Christ, is a collection of supposed secret doctrines received by Moses from the Lord on Mount Sinai. The *G'mara* comprises fuller explanations of the same. The G'mara and Mishnah together constitute the *Talmud* (doctrine). There were two Talmuds: the earlier one, of Jerusalem, and the later, of Babylon.

About the same time, in the second century, the *Kabalah* was developed, which was a medley of Jewish, Pythagorean and Oriental notions. Albert Pike, in his book entitled "Morals and Dogma of the Ancient and Accepted Rite of Scottish Freemasonry," published for the instruction of the Masons of the United States, extols the Kabalah as a principal part of that wonderful revelation which, under the mysterious name of *"the Light"* is made known to the initiates of the highest degrees of that secret society.

The Kabalah is there said to be both a religion and a philosophy. Pike speaks of it in his instructions to the "Prince Adept," or "Knight of the Sun," which is the twenty-eighth degree of Scottish Masonry (p. 744). He says: "All truly dogmatic religions have issued from the Kabalah and return to it. Everything scientific and grand in the religious dreams of all the Illuminati, Jacob Boehme, Swedenborg, Saint Martin and others, is borrowed from the Kabalah. *All the masonic associations owe to it their secrets and symbols* (italics Pike's). The Kabalah alone consecrates the alliance of the universal Reason and the Divine Word; it establishes, by the counterpoise of two forces apparently opposite, the eternal balance of being; it alone reconciles Reason with Faith, Power with Liberty, Science with Mystery; it has the keys of the Present, the Past and the Future. One is filled with admiration on penetrating into the sanctuary of the Kabalah; with which, no doubt, you will make ourselves acquainted as to the creation."

The Kabalistic teaching is briefly analyzed in Henry's translation of the "Epitome of the History of Philosophy, Adopted by the University of France for the Colleges of

that Country" (n. 95), Vol. I, page 220, as follows:
"1. The primary substance is represented as an ocean of
light. The creation, or rather emanation, is represented
as a veil which the infinite light has spread out before
itself and upon which it wrote the forms of things. 2.
There was a primitive emanation, which, under the
name of "Adam Kadmon," is at once the image of God
and the type of man, and from which proceed decreasing
stages of emanations, called Sephiroth. 3. Matter has
only an ideal existence, because it is nothing but the ob-
scuration of the divine rays when arrived at the last
stage of emanation. It is a sort of carbonization of the
divine substance." [1]

ARTICLE II. THE GRÆCO-ORIENTAL SCHOOLS.

46. 1. **The Gnostics** arose in the first century of the
Christian era. They pretended to possess a knowledge
higher and more ancient than that of the Christian revelation. Their system was partly religious and partly
philosophical.

Cerinthus, the refutation of whom St. John seems to
have had in mind when he wrote his Gospel, was an early
Gnostic; another was *Marcion*. When St. Polycarp met
the latter in Rome, and was asked by him whether he

---

[1] These speculations might not seem worthy of our attention, were
it not that the Freemasons, who teach this as the great secret," *The
Light,*" claim a following of eight hundred thousand adult men in
the United States, in the midst of our Christian civilization. The
vast majority of them know not what absurdities are promised them
in the revelation of "The Light."

did not know him, he answered, "I know you to be the first-born of the Devil." These men were not heretics denying some portion of Christianity, but they were not Christians at all: they introduced intermediate beings between God and matter, because they considered it philosophically impossible that the all-perfect God should act directly on matter.

The principal Gnostic of the third century was *Manes*, who renewed the dualistic system of the Persians (n. 9). His followers, called after his name *Manicheans*, continued teaching his errors. In the Middle Ages, under the name of *Albigenses*, they overran portions of France, desecrating and burning churches, murdering priests and religious, till their army was defeated by Simon de Montfort. They still plotted in secret, and it was to protect religion and society against them that the tribunal of the Inquisition was instituted.

47. 2. **Neo-Platonism** was a system in which the religious notions of the East were blended with the speculations of the early Greek philosophers. It was fundamentally a theory of emanations, like Brahmanism; but it was developed scientifically by the admixture of some teachings of Platonism. Another of its characteristics was Oriental mysticism, combined with magic and necromancy.

In its earliest form it was chiefly propagated by *Plotinus* (A.D. 205 to 270). The first being, it teaches, is the *One*, who is also the Good, the Absolute Unity, Simplicity, Infinity. It remains unchanged while there emanates from it what is called a *mind* (νοῦς); because the good must communicate itself. This mind, by turning itself to the One, is differentiated from it. It sees all ideas in itself, differentiating them by noticing them. *The souls* of men emanate from this mind, as the mind emanates from the One. They are individualized by their respective bodies, with which they were united after a former state of higher excellence. All knowledge originates in that mind. The highest happiness of men is in the contemplation of the One. Moral evil consists for the soul in yielding to the body, moral good in emancipating itself from the control of the body by practices of asceticism.

The lofty views which Plotinus entertained of God, the soul, the nature of virtue, etc., gained for him the admiration of many generations, even among the early Christian writers. St. Augustine extols him and Plato above all other philosophers; for he says: "This voice of Plato, the purest and grandest that there is in philosophy, was found once more in the mouth of Plotinus, who was so like him that the one appeared to have risen again in the other" (Con. Acad., III, 41).

Porphyry wrote extensively to explain Plotinus, in which task he displayed great learning and keenness of mind. He was a violent foe to Christianity, as was also his successor Iamblicus.

Iamblicus was the leader of the Syrian Neo-Platonists. He was a strong advocate of polytheism and of the use of magical practices, with which he was so familiar that his followers thought him capable of performing real miracles. His philosophy was one of successive emanations, thus systematically defending the existence of many gods.

Neo-Platonism continued to enjoy much favor with the pagans, because it seemed to harmonize polytheism with philosophy, and was thus their most powerful weapon of defense against the spreading of Christianity. It flourished in Athens and Alexandria, until, in the sixth century, its last able advocates and leaders of the school were themselves converted to the religion of Christ in the persons of *Philiponus* and *Olympiodorus*.

PART II.

PHILOSOPHY OF THE CHRISTIAN ERA.

48. We have seen that the Pre-Christian philosophy had been worn out. While its votaries were occupied in forming various new adaptations and combinations of fragments of rejected systems, **the Gospel truths** began to flood the world with a new, benignant light.

Many great minds soon accepted this higher wisdom in its fullness, and thenceforth used their reason for the twofold purpose of spreading this salutary teaching further and further through the world, and of penetrating deeper into the mysteries thus revealed.

Others, however, continued to make their reason the ultimate judge of every individual truth. The former attitude of mind was prevalent, though not universal, during the first fifteen centuries of the new era; the latter, which may be called the rationalistic, has been prevalent ever since.

The philosophy of the Christian era may suitably be divided into **three periods:**

1. The *Patristic* philosophy, extending to the invasion of the barbarians;

2. The philosophy of the *Middle Ages*, extending thence to the fifteenth century;

3. *Modern* philosophy, extending from the fifteenth century to our own time.

From the invasion of the barbarians till the reconstruction of society, from A.D. about 400 to 800, all was turmoil in Europe; philosophy was ignored: *silent artes inter arma.*

SECTION I.

PATRISTIC PHILOSOPHY.

49. The Blessed Saviour and His Apostles taught dog-
matically as having power to command absolute assent,
as may readily be seen exemplified in the Sermon on the
Mount, in the fifth, sixth, and seventh chapters of St.
Matthew's Gospel. Still even during the lifetime of the
Apostles several heresies, some of which had a philosophic cast, began to spread among Christians.

Some **heretics,** in the spirit of rationalism, strove to
adapt the Christian doctrines to certain ancient systems
of philosophy, as Philo had done with the truths of the
Old Testament. Their errors dealt chiefly with the
Logos, the *Word,* which they made an intermediate being
between God and the world. Others held to the dual-
stic explanation of evil, which they attributed to a creator distinct from God (n. 46). *Monarchianism,* which
admitted but one person in God, and denied the Holy
Trinity, was a reaction against Manicheanism and Gnos-
icism (n. 46). It made the *Logos* extrinsic to the Deity,
yet a good being, who was rewarded with the title of
God, and by whom God created all things. It was partly
with a view to refute this error that St. John began his
Gospel with the statement of the true doctrine, saying:
In the beginning was the Word, and the Word was with

God and the Word was God. The same was in the beginning with God. All things were made by Him; and
without Him was made nothing that was made," etc.

Opposed to all these errors was the philosophy of the
Fathers, that is, of the early theologians of the Church.
Of these some wrote before and others after the General
Council of Nice.

CHAPTER I.

THE ANTE–NICENE FATHERS.

50. The earliest of the Fathers studied no philosophy, but merely explained the doctrines of revelation without proving them by human reasoning. Then came those who wrote for the purpose of defending Christianity against the assaults of pretended philosophers, and who are styled the " **Apologists.**" Of these the principal are:

1. *St. Justin*, the Philosopher and Martyr, A.D. 100 to 160; *Athanagoras*, who died about 180; *Tatian* and *Theophilus*, both before the year 200. All these center their attention on the *Word*, or *Logos* as generated by the Father, yet not separated from Him, eternal and one with Him. Their language is often vague and sometimes incorrect; for they were grappling with deep mysteries which had not yet received a thorough examination by the philosophic mind. Their defense of religion was against the pagans.

2. *St. Irenæus* was a disciple of St. Polycarp, who himself had been instructed by the Apostle St. John. Born in 140, he died a Martyr in 202. He and his disciple *St. Hippolytus* wrote principally against the Gnostics, the Monarchianists and the Marcionites. His refutation of Gnosticism exists in a Latin translation. He shows that in Christianity there is no secret Gnosis, nor

any Demiurgus; but God is directly the Creator of all things; the Logos and the Spirit are one with God, one simple Being. He teaches that God can be known from His works, and that the better minds among the pagans had acquired such knowledge of Him. The law of God is written in the hearts of men; moral evil is not in matter but in our abuse of free will.

3. *Tertullian,* born at Carthage A.D. 160, was converted to Christianity in 190. He became a most zealous and able defender of the true religion against both pagans and heretics. But he erred through excessive rigor so as to fall into open heresy. He may, however, have been reconciled before his death, which occurred A.D. 240.

While the Church has always highly appreciated the services rendered her by Christian writers, it must be borne in mind that her doctrines do not rest on philosophic speculations of any men, as St. Paul emphatically declares throughout the first three chapters of his First Epistle to the Corinthians, saying, for instance: "Christ sent me . . . . to preach the Gospel, not in the wisdom of speech, lest the Cross of Christ should be made void. Where is the wise? where is the scribe? where is the disputer of this world? Has not God made foolish the wisdom of this world? My speech and my preaching was not in the persuasive words of human wisdom, but in the showing of the Spirit and of power, that you might not stand on the wisdom of men but on the power of God," etc.

4. *Clement of Alexandria,* who died in 217, exposed the absurdities of paganism, and drew up a systematic explanation and defense of Christian dogma and morals. He claims all that is good in Greek philosophy to have

come from the *Logos,* or *Word,* "Who enlighteneth every man that cometh into this world" (John I, 9). The true "Gnosis" is the teaching of the Church; the Christian "Gnostic" is the perfect Christian philosopher.

5. *Origen* (185 to 254), a pupil of Clement, taught that the Christian philosopher must take his stand on the teachings of the Church; these he endeavored to explain by views borrowed from Plato, Philo and the Neo-Platonists. He fell into very considerable errors; for instance, he defended the preëxistence of human souls before the birth of men, the eternal existence of the world, the final restoration to grace of all spiritual beings; also the material nature of spirits, to which he assigns a very subtile body.

It is interesting to notice that, while St. Justin, Clement of Alexandria, Origen and St. Augustine, with other Fathers of the Church admired Greek philosophy, and considered it as divinely designed to prepare the world for the Gospel of Christ; Tertullian, Arnobius, Lactantius, who has been surnamed the Christian Cicero, and others considered the same philosophy as opposed to Christianity, and almost as invented by the Devil.

Clement and Origen, while renowned as Apologists of the Faith, also enjoyed a high reputation as lecturers in *the Catechetical school of Alexandria,* where they explained the truths of revelation, forming them into a consistent body of doctrines, and supporting them by philosophical reasonings. From such labors first arose the science of theology.

CHAPTER II.

THE POST-NICENE FATHERS.

51. The Ecumenical Council of Nice, held A.D. 325, the first of the nineteen General Councils of the Church, had drawn up a *Creed* which settled definitely for all Catholics some of the most important teachings both of philosophy and theology. The Creed begins thus: "I believe in one God the Father Almighty, the Maker of heaven and earth, and of all things visible and invisible. And in one Lord Jesus Christ, the only begotten Son of God, born of the Father before all ages, God of God, Light of Light, true God of true God; begotten, not made, consubstantial with the Father, by whom all things were made," etc.

But as the Arians, the Gnostics and other opponents of the Church continued to assail those truths, the defense of them gave occasion to the Post-Nicene Fathers to write learned treatises on philosophical questions, such, for instance, as regarded the relation between the Logos and the Father, the nature of personality, of the creation, etc.

The principal of these Fathers were, among the Greeks, *St. Athanasius*, the Patriarch of Alexandria, and the three Capadocian Saints *Gregory of Nyssa, Basil* and *Gregory of Nazianzum;* and, among the Latins, Saints *Hilary, Ambrose, Jerome* and *Augustine*. All of these

Fathers lived between A.D. 350 and 450. Most of their writings are theological; still philosophical matters are often treated in them. St. Augustine deserves our chief attention.

52. Born at Tagaste in Numidia, **Augustine** studied and taught rhetoric at Carthage, where he upheld the errors of the Manicheans. Converted afterwards at Milan by St. Ambrose, he nobly repaired the scandalous conduct of his youth, and became the holy bishop of Hippo Regius, in Africa, and one of the greatest glories of the Church. In his many learned works he explains and defends the Christian doctrine with the aid of the Neo-Platonic philosophy. **His teachings** may be summarized as follows:

1. *God* is one, supreme, most perfect, eternal, immutable and omnipresent; who knew all things before they existed, not knowing them because they are, but (except free acts, of course) they are because He knows them; the Divine intellect comprises the prototypes, or exemplars of all things.

2. *The world*, being composed of finite and variable things, is evidently not self-existent, but produced from nothing, created. Therefore God is a Being entirely distinct from the world, and not the soul of the world; for otherwise everything would be a part of God, which is absurd. Besides, since nothing can control the will of God, the motive why God created the world is His will alone; and since a perfect God cannot create anything but what is good, evil does not come from Him directly but from the finite nature of things.

3. *The soul* is immaterial, because it perceives immaterial things. It is, at least virtually, entire in the whole

body and in every part of the body, because at all points
it perceives impressions where they occur. It is certain
of its own existence; for if it doubted of it, this doubt
itself would prove it to exist. It is immortal because
it is capable of knowing immutable and eternal truths.

This brief sketch of St. Augustine's philosophy does
not furnish a fair appreciation of that extraordinary
man. His great mind gathered together all the elements
of Christian philosophy till then called into existence,
reduced them to unity, and left to succeeding ages a vast,
systematic body of truths. Not that he pretended to
have found the answer to every question of the human
mind; he freely acknowledged his ignorance on many
points. But he displays, as Stoeckl expresses it, "such
depth of thought, such delicacy of discrimination, a
spirit of inquiry so fruitful in results, such a genuine appreciation of the ideal, such conclusive reasoning, as are
not often found in one man to the same degree. God
and the soul—these were the objects to which his investi-
gations were chiefly directed; the whole effort of his mind
found expression in the pregnant words *Noverim Te,
noverim me,* 'Let me know Thee (O Lord), let me know
myself'" (Finlay, p. 265).

53. The invasion of the barbarians, which began soon
after A.D. 400, in a brief time put an end to all study.
The torch of philosophy kept on flickering in the writings
of a very few truly distinguished men, such as *Boëthius*
(470 to 526); *Cassiodorus* (468 to 535); *St. John Damas-
cene,* who toward the end of the seventh century explained Aristotle's Dialectics and Ontology; *the Pseudo-
Dionysius,* who was for many ages supposed to be
identical with Dionysius the Areopagite converted by St.

Paul at Athens (Acts xvii), and who treated Christianity in connection with the principles of Neo-Platonism; *St. Isidore* of Seville, in the seventh century, and *Venerable Bede* in England (674 to 735).

We will conclude this section with a brief notice of *Boëthius*. He was a Roman senator, who lived at the court of King Theodoric, by whom he was unjustly condemned to death. He forms a bright link in the chain which connects the philosophy of antiquity with that of the Middle Ages. An earnest student of Plato and Aristotle, and no less earnest a Christian, he produced, besides many valuable translations of ancient masterpieces, some truly classical works of his own, which were for many subsequent ages the delight of scholars. Conspicuous among these is the book which he wrote in prison and styled the "Consolations of Philosophy." It presents a Christian eclecticism from the best systems of antiquity; and is, as it were, the last testament of his noble mind, left to enrich future generations.

SECTION II.

MEDIEVAL PHILOSOPHY.

54. The philosophy generally taught in the universities of the Middle Ages is called the **Philosophy of the Schools,** or **Scholastic Philosophy.** It consists in a constant effort to harmonize with one another the doctrines of revelation and the teachings of reason. The Scholastic philosopher professes to be guided by these two principles, *intelligo ut credam* and *credo ut intelligam*, I understand so as to believe" and "I believe so as to understand"; that is, reason bids me believe the Church teaching, and faith aids my reason in two ways: it guards my speculations from the wanderings of error in the field of natural knowledge, and it opens up to me further regions of knowledge.

The Schools here spoken of were at first very modest efforts made to light up the dark night of ignorance which the barbarian invaders had spread like a pall over all Europe. The work was slow in the beginning, then rapid, next brilliant, till it declined in brightness and usefulness. We have thus *four periods* of Medieval philosophy, namely the periods of *formation, development, perfection* and *decline*.

CHAPTER I.

THE PERIOD OF FORMATION.

FROM A.D. 400 TO 1050.

55. While the bright light of Christianity was rapidly spreading from Rome over the greater portion of Europe, a very dark cloud was drifting from the North southward in the **invasion of numerous barbarian races.** In A.D. 407 the Vandals invaded Gaul, Burgundy and Spain, finally settling in Africa, where they destroyed all civilization; in 410 Alaric with his Goths sacked the city of Rome itself, which was three times plundered in sixty years. Some fifty years later Attila with his Huns followed in his tracks, devastating chiefly Germany and France. Meanwhile came the Franks, who settled in Gaul, the Angles and Saxons, who invaded Britain, and the Visigoths, who took possession of Spain and the Southern portions of Gaul. All these invaders, except perhaps the Franks, destroyed whatever civilization and learning existed wherever they settled or passed; so that the fifth, sixth, seventh and eighth centuries are deservedly styled Dark Ages.

Yet *Italy*, under the immediate influence of the Popes, had never totally abandoned the study of literature and philosophy, nor, of course, of theology; Virgil, Cicero, St. Augustine, Boëthius and Cassiodorus, besides the Holy Scriptures, were read in the schools, not of the clergy alone, but also of the people.

In *France* little was taught the secular youths except religion, war and courtly manners. Charlemagne was there the first to found literary schools, in which reading, writing and the rudiments of grammar at first made up the whole curriculum. He had lived a while in Italy, and it was probably during his stay there that he resolved to encourage letters in his own domains.

His teachers came mostly from Ireland, which country had preserved a knowledge and love of Greek and Latin literature and the traditions of other kinds of ancient learning. In fact the education thus introduced into France was called *Irish learning*.

Still the noted scholar who first began to teach letters in France was not an Irishman by birth, but the Englishman *Alcuin*, who had studied at York. He was, however, assisted by *Clement* and other Irish scholars. Alcuin was the organizer and promoter of the new institutions of learning, and taught in them personally from 781 to 804. When the curriculum became fully organized, it comprised two divisions: the *trivium*, consisting of grammar, rhetoric and dialectics; and the *quadrivium*, that is, arithmetic, geometry, astronomy and music.

The only philosopher of name during this formative period was the very talented but eccentric *Scotus Erigena*. He attempted to combine theology and philosophy into one harmonious system; but, though a sincere Christian at heart, he only succeeded in producing a novel system of pantheism, which is described by his contemporary Gerbert as rivaling in grandeur and gigantic character the bold creations of Indian philosophy. But, since truth, and not originality, is the real test of the value of a philosophy, his system was worthless.

This genius flourished in the middle of the ninth century.

Another philosopher of this period was *Gerbert*, c Aquitaine, who in 999 became Pope under the name o Sylvester II. He is said to have been the first to intro duce Arabic numbers among Christian peoples, and t have constructed clocks and other ingenious mechan isms. He was an acute disputant, and composed th first treatise which compared the *pros* and *cons* of a ques tion after a fashion that became very common amon subsequent Scholastic writers.

This period of formation was remarkable for *the estal lishment of many schools* in Ireland, England, France Germany, Italy, Belgium, Spain and other countries Wherever, in fact, monasteries were founded, or bishop had their sees, there arose institutions of learning. Sev eral of them had three or more thousands of scholars who flocked to them even from distant lands, and wer generally taught gratis, often even supplied with th necessaries of life. Thus originated many centers of er lightenment, some of which have continued to exist du ing all the intervening ages till the present time.

Among these schools the Irish were the oldest and th most numerously attended. Such were those of A magh, Arran, Clonard, Clon-mac-noise, Clonfert, Bango Birr, Lismore, Cashel and others. From Ireland mi sionaries of religion and teachers of literature an philosophy went forth to convert and civilize, by estal lishing churches, monasteries and schools, probably i every country of Europe. (See an article on "Histor of Schools," by Rev. William Poland, S.J., in the *America Catholic Quarterly Review* for April, 1903.)

CHAPTER II.

GROWTH OF SCHOLASTICISM.

FROM A.D. 1050 TO 1200.

56. The philosophic discussions of this period often turn upon the nature of **Universals,** a question which from that time to the present day has occupied the minds of countless disputants. *The question is this:* "What objective reality corresponds to our universal ideas, such as animal, man, body, substance, cause, effect, etc.?" Scotus Erigena, as a follower of Plato, had supposed the real existence of universal objects outside the mind (n. 24). This now was denied by *Roscelin,* who wrote some two hundred and fifty years later; he died about A.D. 1100. He truthfully maintained that universal objects could not exist as such; but he went too far in the opposite direction, and taught that even our ideas are not universal; all we have, he said, were general names, thus founding the school of *Nominalism.*

This is one of the most important questions in philosophy, inasmuch as our knowledge is not true unless it be conformable to the objective reality. If we have no universal ideas, then we can have no general principles, and therefore no science. If we have universal ideas but no object at all exists for them out of the mind, then our knowledge is false, because not conformable to the reality. Aristotle had solved the difficulty by teaching that we have truly universal ideas and that the objects corresponding to them out of our minds are the common natures of classes, or species, of things. For instance, our universal idea "animal" represents whatever traits or notes are common to all animals, and is realized in each animal (n. 27). But of Aristotle's works the Christian schools possessed at the time only *De Interpretatione* and the *Categoriæ*. Boëthius had transmitted the true explanation; but it was not generally noticed.

Starting thus from false principles, Roscelin was led into false, and even heretical conclusions; and, though he was a sincere Christian, and was not obstinate in his errors, still his mistakes created confusion of minds, and for a time made dialectics odious.

The confusion was increased by *William of Champeau* (1070–1121), who, if he has been correctly reported by his opponent Abélard, considered the universals as existing out of the mind and existing as universals; not in an ideal world, as Plato had supposed, but in our own world. For instance, an animal was a universal animal, one with every other existing animal, except in accidents. This doctrine would logically lead to monism. Probably William did not mean this; but his terms were infelicitous.

57. **St. Anselm** (1033–1109), born in Piedmont, became the renowned Archbishop of Canterbury, in England. He wrote various philosophical and theological treatises, as occasions happened to require; but, besides this, he built up a philosophic system, of which the main features regard God, the Word of God and the liberty of the human soul.

1. *The existence of God* he proves by various valid ar-

guments, especially by the necessity of a First Cause and of an intelligent Ordainer; but, besides this, he invented the *ontological* argument, which has made much noise in the philosophic world. It may be stated briefly as follows: We have an idea of an infinitely perfect being; but an infinitely perfect being is necessarily an existing being; for if it were not existing it would not be infinitely perfect; therefore an infinitely perfect being exists. What really follows from the premises is that we have an idea of a being which must exist, if our idea is objectively true. The argument may be put in various forms, one more deceptive than the other, but never so as to be valid.

2. St. Anselm attempts to prove by reason alone that *the Word* must exist in God, saying: God from eternity must have had perfect knowledge of Himself and of all possible things; but the knowledge of an infinite mind must be expressed by an infinite Word, which is one with God and yet proceeds from God; and, moreover, there must be an infinite love between those two Persons, which is the Holy Ghost. All this is true and beautiful, but without revelation it would not give us certainty.

3. *The freedom of the human will* is defended by St. Anselm with much ingenuity and dignity, but not with perfect correctness; for his explanation cannot well be reconciled with the preservation of man's freedom after the fall of Adam.

58. The most noted philosopher of this period was the brilliant but erratic **Pierre Abélard** (about 1079 to 1142), who, when a mere youth, drew crowds of eager disciples around him at Paris, and, later in life, in various other places. Intoxicated with his success he presumed to

make his own mind the measure of truth, even in matters of revelation, rejecting such doctrines as stood in the way of his speculations. He refused to believe in mysteries, saying: to what purpose would God reveal mysteries to us if we cannot understand them? His unorthodox teachings on the Holy Trinity and other dogmas were condemned in 1140. His pride met with a disgraceful fall in connection with the notorious Héloïse; but it would appear that both atoned by public penance for the public scandal. He opposed William of Champeau on the question of universals; but his own views on the matter are not clear.

59. **Peter the Lombard** (1100–1160), styled *the Master of the Sentences*, published a most useful work called "The Four Books of Sentences," a collection of the teachings of the Fathers on questions of Catholic doctrine, which was for several centuries the common text-book of the schools. It was made the subject of innumerable commentaries, so that it was in the thirteenth century the core of scholastic literature.

The religious errors into which Roscelin and Abélard had been led by their philosophic speculations produced in the school of the Abbey of St. Victor, near Paris, a considerable distrust of dialectics; and influenced the teachers there to maintain that the soul cannot attain the purposes of philosophy by reason alone, but must be elevated to this attainment by direct communings with God, by what is called *Mysticism*. Usually **Mysticism** had been the tendency of pantheistic philosophers; but on this occasion it became, under proper limitations and with due moderation, the doctrine of the orthodox writers *Hugh of St. Victor* and his successor *Richard,* of the same abbey. These were men of deep and sincere piety, who wrote with much unction and considerable learning. Their spirit of union with God in prayer and study was fostered by the discourses and writings of their great contemporary *St. Bernard* (1091 to 1153). But *Walter of St. Victor* went much too far in his opposition to dialectics.

60. In the latter half of the twelfth century, **a school of philosophers at Chartres**, in France, advocated some altogether heretical theories, systems, in fact, of downright pantheism. They falsely pretended to follow Aristotle, whose treatises on Physics and Metaphysics had lately been translated from the Arabic into Latin. The ecclesiastical authorities at Paris, supposing the new errors to be really derived from Aristotle's writings, forbade the use of these works at the schools of the city, until the errors which had been connected with them were found to be foreign accretions to his doctrines; when the prohibition was withdrawn.

In 1254 the exposition of the Aristotelian Physics and Metaphysics was sanctioned by the University of Paris, and the sway of Aristotle's mind over the Christian schools was finally established. Just as the "Sentences" of Peter Lombard formed the groundwork of theological instruction, so the writings of Aristotle became the basis of all philosophical teaching. Aristotle was spoken of as *the philosopher*. Hence the numerous commentaries on him by the Schoolmen became the treasury and the glory of Scholastic philosophy.

61. We have just referred to the Arabic translators of Aristotle. **The Arabians** had received Aristotle's works at an early date from the Syrian and Persian Christians,

who in 539 had sheltered the Greek philosophers then
banished from Athens by the Emperor Justinian.   After
the Arabians had become Mahometans, they cared only
for the learning of the Koran, till the middle of the eighth
century.   Then dissidents arose among them, who soon
began to build their speculations, first on Neo-Platonism,
and afterwards on Aristotle.

The ablest of their philosophers were *Avincenna* (980–
1037) and *Averroës* (1127–1198), both of whom defended
Aristotle against the mysticism of their countrymen.
The latter author says: "Aristotle's doctrine is the highest truth, because his intellect was the *ne plus ultra* of the
human intellect."   The Arabians, however, misrepre-
sented some of these teachings in their commentaries,
and they seem to have even mistranslated the works
themselves.   Among the many errors of Averroës was
his view of the human intellect, which he took to be an
impersonal power, one in all men, and immortal, while
there was no immortality for each individual soul.

It was against this error that Albert the Great, in 1256,
wrote his treatise "On the Unity of the Intellect Against
Averroës," and St. Thomas "On the Unity of the Intellect Against the Averroïsts."   These *Averroïsts* were
Christians, who, to escape the condemnation of the
Church, pretended that what they defended as true in
philosophy might be false in theology, so that they should
not be interfered with.

62. During this same period many **Jews** also devoted
themselves to the study of philosophy; *Moses Maimonides*
was the greatest of their Aristotelians (1135–1204).   In
the Moorish portions of Spain the Jews enjoyed at the
time special advantages; for in the same region the Ma-

hometans had not yet begun to tolerate such studies among themselves. They translated the Greek authors into Hebrew, from which language the Christians rendered them into Latin. Soon after, however, the Greek texts were brought from the East into the Christian schools, and correct copies and good Latin translations were thus secured.

CHAPTER III.

PERFECTION OF SCHOLASTICISM.

From a.d. 1200 to 1300.

63. The most renowned philosophers of this period were the following:

1. *Alexander of Hales*, born in England, was the first Franciscan Father who lectured at the Paris University, where the secular clergy had till then held exclusive sway. He was also the first author who wrote there after the introduction of all Aristotle's works. He composed a *Summa of Universal Theology*, giving it the form which was afterwards adopted by St. Thomas Aquinas; namely, first laying down the objections against a thesis, then the proof of it, and next refuting the objections. He strove, with only partial success, to combine the teachings of Aristotle with those of St. Augustine, which had so far been dominant in the schools. The great work which he accomplished was the outlining of the plan followed after him in all the great "Summæ." He died in 1245. He has been styled *Doctor Irrefragabilis*.

2. *William of Paris*, who died in 1249, wrote philosophical treatises "On the Universe" and "On the Soul," in which he displays a very keen intellect and much erudition. He had completely mastered the systems of Plato, Aristotle and the Arabian philosophers. These last he refuted with distinguished ability and success.

3. *Vincent de Beauvais,* who died A.D. 1264, in a work which he entitled "A Mirror," *Speculum,* gave to the world an encyclopedia of all the learning of his day.

4. *St. Bonaventure, Doctor Seraphicus,* a pupil of Hales and a Franciscan like him, began his lectures in the Paris University the same year as St. Thomas Aquinas, A.D. 1257. He became the general of the Franciscan Order, and was made a Cardinal by Gregory X. He was the leader of the Franciscan School, as St. Thomas was of the Dominican. Although they were constantly united by the bonds of a holy friendship, they differed on important points of philosophy and theology. In particular the Franciscans taught the plurality of forms in plants and animals, which the Thomistic School denied. St. Bona-venture leans to the mysticism of Hugh of St. Victor (n. 60). Both he and St. Thomas died the same year, 1274.

5. *Roger Bacon, Doctor Mirabilis,* born in 1214, first studied at Paris, then at Oxford, became a Franciscan and one of the most famous professors of that university. He entered on that method of observation and experiment which, three centuries later, gained so much favor for his namesake Lord Bacon. Brilliant and bold in his speculations, but destitute of proper respect for authority, he wandered into deplorable errors. In particular he admitted no deductive, but only inductive reasoning. While he made important scientific discoveries, he destroyed his influence by the extravagance of some of his claims, and eventually rendered but little permanent service to science and philosophy.

6. *Blessed Albert the Great, the Universal Doctor* (1193–1280), had mastered a wonderful knowledge considering

the times he lived in; for he possessed all the learning of that age, and, along with it, he had acquired an insight into the natural sciences far beyond the reach of his contemporaries. In philosophy he carefully selected all the best teachings of Plato and Aristotle, and also gave due credit to the Jews and the Arabians, freely criticising every doctrine as he handled it. While lacking in the special talent required to build up a compact system, he prepared for his pupil St. Thomas the elements of his future works.

7. *St. Thomas of Aquin*, the Angelic Doctor (1225–1274), the glory of the Friars Preachers and of all the Church, was the greatest of all writers on philosophy and theology combined. To analyze his teachings adequately would require a good-sized volume; in fact ordinary text-books on these two sciences in Catholic schools to-day are chiefly compendiums of the doctrines which are scattered through his numerous works. Besides many minor treatises, which are now usually collected under the title *Questiones Disputatæ* (Mooted Questions), and *Questiones Quotlibetales* (Miscellaneous Questions), he composed two extensive works, "The Summa Against the Gentiles," which is a complete vindication, or apology, of the Church against the charges of non-Christians, and the *Summa Theologica*, the summing up of all his philosophical and theological learning. The former has lately been translated into English, under the title of "God and His Creatures," by Rev. Joseph Rickaby, S. J.

In particular St. Thomas teaches on philosophic matters as follows:

1. Science is the knowledge of things through their causes. 2. Theology and philosophy differ essentially

by their formal objects; that is, they view the matters created differently; philosophy views them by the light of reason, theology by the light of faith. Since both these lights come from God, these sciences cannot conflict with one another. 3. Science can aid faith in several ways: (*a*) By furnishing motives of credibility; (*b*) by supplying analogies; (*c*) by solving objections. On the other hand, faith can aid reason by cautioning it against error, and by enlarging the field of knowledge. 4. All science deals, not with individuals, but with universals. 5. The universals exist as ideas or exemplars in the mind of the Creator, and are formed in the human mind by abstraction from individual things. 6. Not all the sciences furnish the same kind of certainty.

Two doctrines of St. Thomas were vigorously opposed, especially by the Franciscans; namely, the unity of the substantial form in man, and the denial of *rationes seminales*, that is, of certain principles created together with matter, and coöperating with the agent in the production of the effect.

8. *John Duns Scotus*, who taught from 1294 to 1308 at Oxford and Paris, was the brightest luminary among the Franciscans; but he was a meteor rather than a sun. He is deservedly called "the Subtle Doctor," *Doctor Subtilis*, because he is the keenest of critics, finding flaws in all systems; but he is hard to follow in his subtle disquisitions. With all his brilliancy, he has added nothing of importance to the science of philosophy. The Franciscan writers followed him, under the name of *Scotists*, in opposition to the *Thomists*, or followers of St. Thomas.

9. *Raymond Lully*, "the Enlightened Doctor," *Doctor*

Illuminatus, was most active in refuting Averroïsm
While zealously devoting his missionary labors to the
conversion of the Moors, he was stoned at Tunis in 1315
He made the mistake of maintaining that we need the
light of faith to enable our reason to start even in its
efforts for the attainment of the highest truths. He was
so ingenious as to invent a logical machine, which by
means of geometrical figures combined letters as elements of thought into the expression of arguments. He
was so much admired by some that chairs were established at Barcelona and Valentia to perpetuate his enlightened wisdom; while by others he was considered
as unorthodox; and this fact seems to have been the chief
reason why he was not canonized.

CHAPTER IV.

DECLINE OF SCHOLASTICISM.

From a.d. 1300 to 1453.

64. **The purpose of Scholasticism** had been all along to build up an harmonious system of philosophy and theology combined, in which each of these sciences should rest on its own basis, reason and revelation respectively, and the truths proclaimed by one should nowhere be in contradiction with those maintained by the other. For this harmony of the two sciences is the very idea and definition of Scholasticism.

This structure had now been completed; it was Scholasticism in its perfection. Within each of these sciences there were disputed points, which gave occasion for the formation of different schools; the *Thomists* and the *Scotists* were the principal of these, but not the only ones. *Universals* continued to be much discussed between *Nominalists*, *Conceptualists* and *Moderate Realists*. *Mysticism*, too, both of the orthodox and of the pantheistic variety, found its defenders in several doctors. But on the whole the discussions had lost their main purpose, that of harmonizing faith and reason; and they became more and more trifling, minute and useless, degenerating from their former importance and dignity.

When we call this *a period of decline*, it is not to indicate that truth was diminished among the learned, or

false views had become prevalent; but the form of dis-
cussing the truths was perverted in various ways: 1.
The language became more and more uncouth, harsh and
deficient in literary ornament. 2. Arguments for and
against a thesis were multiplied and drawn out beyond
all reasonable measure. 3. Each disputant often seemed
to fight for the honor of his school rather than for the
triumph of the truth. These tendencies went on in-
creasing till odium became attached to Scholasticism
itself; and they gave occasion to the enemies of sound
doctrine to heap ridicule on its defenders.

65. While the learned generally, during this period,
possessed the truth in peace, disputing only about unimportant points in matters of detail, a few conspicuous
leaders of thought wandered away from the highroad of
sound doctrine; the principal of whom were *Durand* and
William of Ocham. *Durand,* a Dominican professor at
Paris, styled *Doctor Resolutissimus,* was a bold thinker
and writer, who attacked various theses which he failed
to understand aright; yet he happily kept within the
limits of revealed truth. He has been called the Locke
of Scholastic philosophers, because, like Locke, he was
an earnest, well-meaning but superficial critic. After
making much noise but accomplishing little good, he
died in 1332.

William of Ocham, an Englishman (1280–1349?), *Doctor Invincibilis,* was a rash and bitter opponent of Thom-
ism, and of the temporal power of the popes. He revived Nominalism, or rather changed it into *Conceptualism,* teaching that we have universal ideas, but denying
all universality in the objects; and he made various other
mistakes of no small moment. For instance, he denied

that reason can demonstrate the immortality of the soul, the existence, unity and infinity of God, or the creation of the world. During the fourteenth century Nominalism had some able defenders; but the body of the Schoolmen remained faithful to Moderate Realism.

66. The idle discussion of interminable questions disgusted at the time many earnest lovers of truth and virtue, and led them to abandon intellectual philosophy, and devote themselves to a life of contemplation and union with God. *John Ruysbroek* was the founder of this school of Mysticism. His pupil *Gerhart de Groot* founded the *Brothers of the Common Life,* who for some generations were most pious teachers of youth in Germany, Belgium, Holland and other countries, until they were swept away by the storm of the Reformation.

The best known among these Brothers was *Thomas a Kempis* (1380–1471), whose celebrated book, "The Imitation of Christ" is the most convincing proof that the highest wisdom may be attained by men of genuine piety and common sense without much abstract speculation. As a specimen of his manner of philosophizing see Book I, Chapters I, II, III.

Chancellor Gerson, of the Paris University, called *Doctor Christianissimus* (about 1364–1429), was the most distinguished and influential among the orthodox mystics. *Denis the Carthusian, Doctor Ecstaticus,* was another of their brilliant lights. *Henry Suso* (1300–1365) wrote with uncommon gentleness and piety, so as to gain the hearts of all.

But from the fact that the Mystics undervalued close and accurate reasoning, many of them fell into great errors, some even into pantheism, as did *John of Gand.*

John de Mirecourt and *Guido de Medonta.* Others had at
least a taint of unsoundness about them. Such were
Master Eckhart (1260–1361) and *John Tauler* (1290–
1361), both of whom remained indeed within the Church,
but they had little regard for ecclesiastical authority.
Their errors were both philosophical and theological,
concerning chiefly the nature of God and the soul's relations to God.

SECTION III.

MODERN PHILOSOPHY.

67. While philosophy in its enfeebled condition had lost its interest for most of the thoughtful minds of the fifteenth century, it happened that many Greek scholars were driven from the East by the advancing tide of the Moslem invasion. By these a general enthusiasm was enkindled in the West of Europe in favor of a revival, or **Renaissance,** of the study of Greek and Latin literature and the fine arts generally. More attention began to be bestowed on elegant form of expression than on soundness of thought; and the natural beauty so prized by the ancient pagans was soon preferred by many of the literati to the supernatural treasures of Christian literature. From the fact that they extolled mere human excellency as the *summum bonum* in education, the name of *Humanists* was given to the new scholars. They gained further popularity by heaping ridicule and contempt on Scholastic treatises and disputations. The blame was often somewhat deserved; but the mistake was usually made of imputing to the philosophy the shortcomings of the philosophers who at the time defended it.

We shall divide the section on Modern Philosophy into **three portions,** corresponding to three periods: 1. The period of transition, from the fall of Constantinople, in A.D. 1454 to the year 1600. 2. The period from Descartes to Kant, from 1600 to 1780; and 3. From Kant to the present year 1909.

CHAPTER I.

THE TRANSITION PERIOD.

FROM A.D. 1454 TO 1600.

68. The earnest study of philosophy in connection with theology continued uninterrupted in Italy, Spain and Portugal, and produced there during this period some of the richest fruits of human learning. In particular, extensive and most able commentaries were then written on the works of St. Thomas and Duns Scotus, masterpieces that remain the admiration and the treasure of students till the present day. The principal of them were composed by *Cardinal Cajetan*, who lived from 1469 to 1534; by *Melchior Cano*, from 1509 to 1560; *Bañez*, 1528 to 1604; and by the Jesuits *Vasquez*, 1531 to 1604, *Fonseca*, 1528 to 1599, and *Suarez*, 1548 to 1617. The works of the last-named philosopher and theologian comprise twenty-three volumes in folio.

After printing was invented in 1440, books multiplied exceedingly, and thus a strong impulse was given to general enlightenment, and not less to pride of intellect in many scholars. Even the Holy Scriptures were criticised by some as too deficient in beauty of style to be read without prejudice to pure Latinity. Large numbers, both of the clergy and laity, spent much time in exalting and imitating the pagan models, to the serious neglect of sacred learning and other more important duties.

The Humanists, together with Plato's cultured style, also brought back his philosophic system. This was done by *Cardinal Bessarion*, a Greek (1400–1457); while the two brothers *John* and *Francis Pico della Mirandola* fiercely attacked the followers of Aristotle. *Justus Lipsius* revived Stoicism; *Paracelsus*, the reformer of the medical science, introduced a mixture of chemistry and theosophy; *Montaigne* and *Charron* promoted Scepticism.

Giordano Bruno (1548–1600) maintained the perfect identity of nature and God. An apostate and a violent enemy of Christianity, he traveled through various lands, everywhere arousing the indignation of Catholics and Protestants alike, till at last he returned to Rome, where he was publicly burned as a rebel against Church and State. It is owing to this pitiful death that he has of late been idolized by the enemies of the Pope.

69. *Francis Bacon* (1561–1626), who became Lord Chancellor of England with the title of Baron Verulam, inaugurated the scientific movement of the inductive study of nature. His chief work is called *Instauratio Magna*, and claims to be a general reconstruction of science. The part of it which is styled *Novum Organum* explains the inductive process as a new tool of the mind by which knowledge can be acquired, and which had never before been properly explained to men. True Aristotle had treated of it, but he had not revealed its entire efficacy. The real important service rendered by Bacon to mankind was not one invention or another, but a new direction given to the investigation of truth, namely by the personal and close observation of nature. Roger Bacon and Albert the Great had inaugurated the movement, Lord Bacon rendered it popular; that is all

he did. (Regarding the excess of praise lavished on him, see *American Catholic Quarterly Review* for January, 1908, pages 138, etc.)

He also insisted earnestly on the necessity of removing from the mind preconceived opinions never before carefully submitted to examination. He classes such prejudices into distinct categories, namely: (*a*) *Idols of the tribe,* that is, false notions common to the whole human race; (*b*) *idols of the den,* errors arising from peculiarities of character; (*c*) *idols of the marketplace,* from our own associations; (*d*) *idols of the theater,* from traditional teachings. No doubt most of our prejudices arise from one of these sources, and it was useful to call attention to them. But the same had often been done by others for instance, Roger Bacon had pointed out the following four sources of prejudices: (*a*) Trusting inadequate authorities; (*b*) the force of custom; (*c*) confiding in the opinion of the inexperienced; (*d*) hiding one's ignorance with the parade of a superficial wisdom. Lord Bacon also made the mistake of assailing the value of deductive, or syllogistic reasoning, against which he created a most unjust prejudice, which has been perpetuated till now in many superficial minds.

70. By this time **Protestantism** had arisen, and with it protracted warfare in several lands, with great injury to scientific studies in almost all civilized countries. However, the Reformation did not make an immediate change in the systems of philosophy taught in the universities. In these, traditional Aristotelianism long held its honored place, in a form, however, adapted by Melanchthon to the needs of Protestant dogma. Meanwhile hostile attacks on Peripateticism continued and

grew more violent. Besides the objections brought against its followers by the Humanists, Protestants as such generally looked upon it as a strong bulwark of the Catholic Church, of traditional orthodoxy and of authority in religion.

Jacob Boehme (1575–1624) is the chief representative of Protestant Mysticism. Before him, *Frank* and *Weigel* had formed such systems; but Boehme carried this method of thought to its most extreme consequences. He was a totally uneducated man, whose ignorance was all the more mischievous on account of his extraordinary earnestness and infatuation. He based his system on visions of God obtained by prayer. God constitutes the essence of all things, he maintained, and contains good and evil. Nature is the body of God, the stars are its organs and their orbits its arteries. His vagaries did not deserve the serious notice of the philosophers; but as he wrote in the language of the people, the German tongue, he greatly increased the confusion of thought then existing in his country.

71. During this same period **Political Philosophy** had attracted the attention of the learned all the more generally as it led to more practical consequences.

1. *Nicolo Machiavelli* (1469–1527), in his work *Il Principe*, had produced a political philosophy of *State Utilitarianism*, which assailed Christian principles, teaching that, when it is a question of saving one's country, there must be no hesitation on the score of justice or injustice, cruelty or kindness, etc. This was a partial application of the false principle that the end may justify the means.

2. Very different was the spirit manifested by *Blessed*

Thomas More (1478-1535) in his *Utopia*, in which he describes an imaginary republic so governed as to secure happiness for all its members. From the title of that work the present meaning of the word "Utopia" has been derived, namely an imaginary condition of life beautiful in theory but impossible in practice. Made by King Henry VIII Lord Chancellor of England, he refused to acknowledge that tyrant as spiritual head of the Church in his dominions, and in consequence was made a martyr for the faith.

3. *Thomas Hobbes* (1588-1679) reaffirmed the old error of Nominalism. He was also a materialist, a sensist, and a subjectivist inasmuch as he denied the objective qualities of things perceived. He taught, for instance, that color exists in the perceiver only, not in the objective reality. There is certainly in objects of sense the power to cause various sensations in the perceiver. His political theory is that of the *Social Contract*, namely, that every man is naturally at war with all other men: *Homo homini lupus;* therefore, to protect themselves against others, men have agreed to vest their rights in the State. The State's power is absolute; the will of the ruler is sovereign law, above any right of conscience or religion.

4. *Hugo Grotius*, or *De Groot* (1557-1628) is the father of the science of *International Law*, which he styles *Jus Gentium*. Though correct on most principles, he advocated novel and erroneous views on the separation of Church and State, on religious liberty, etc.

72. It will be noticed that this **period of the Renaissance** did not produce any grand system of philosophy. Owing especially to the invention of printing, it had given a general impulse to mental action in the common

people; and, owing to the influx of Greek scholars, it had improved elegance of style in literature and widened appreciation of the fine arts; but it had not prompted the learned to cultivate deep and solid thought. It had, however, greatly promoted the physical sciences. It had also pulled down much that was antiquated and useless, and removed many false notions; but not without introducing many others often far more injurious. It claimed to have done wonders, to have, in fact, produced a total rebirth of civilization; but the claim was an idle boast. All this will be easily realized if one reads the late work of Dr. James J. Walsh entitled "The Thirteenth the Greatest of Centuries."

CHAPTER II.

FROM DESCARTES TO KANT.

FROM 1600 TO 1780.

ARTICLE I. CARTESIANISM.

73. René Descartes, in Latin *Cartesius* (1596–1650), though he had been trained by the Jesuits in the Scholastic philosophy, and remained through life a good friend of his former professors, presumed to ignore the accumulated wisdom of the ages, and to build the whole structure of philosophy anew. He thus became the acknowledged founder of *Modern Philosophy*. The spirit of his system consists in questioning the reliability of the first dictates of reason, and in attempting to prove the primary truths while they need no proof, for man cannot reasonably doubt them. Starting with the reasoning *Cogito, ergo sum,* "I think, therefore I exist," he claims that he thus validly establishes his own existence. Finding in his mind the clear idea of God, he concludes from it the existence of God. And from the perfections of the Creator, he argues that the faculties which the Creator has given him must be reliable. But all through this reasoning, he has been taking his understanding to be reliable; he thus moves in a vicious circle. The main error of Descartes and his followers is that they arbitrarily accept some truths as certain and doubt others which are equally evident.

Besides this inconsistency, his system combines a great variety of **other serious errors.** For instance, he mistakes thought, which is only an accident of the mind, for the essence of the mind, and extension for the total essence of matter. Now, since thought and extension have nothing in common, he concludes therefrom that the soul and the body cannot act on each other. A fluid, called *Spiritus animales*, conveys the sense stimuli to the pineal gland, and, returning through the nerves to the muscles, conveys the impulse of motion to the limbs. In brutes there is no feeling of this; they are only automata. In man the soul perceives the affection and acts in consequence.

While most of our ideas are "adventitious," obtained through the senses, or "factitious," made up by ourselves, we have natural dispositions to form certain other ideas which he calls "innate." He rejects the entire Scholastic doctrine of "matter and form," and admits in bodies only motions of material particles from which all their activity results.

Descartes's teaching directly influenced the philosophy of the leading writers in France and other lands for over a century after his death; and indirectly it has perverted modern philosophy till the present day.

If he has been extolled as a great philosopher, it is *not* because he discovered any valuable truth; in fact, his entire system has long since been abandoned by the learned world, and it is utterly inconsistent with the present state of science. But he was admired on account of his boldness and originality in breaking away from the old landmarks. Truth was of less value to him than novelty. Besides, Aristotelianism was considered to be concordant and intimately united with Catholicity; therefore the non-Catholic world heartily welcomed a departure from it.

74. The principles of Descartes received further developments at the hands of some of his disciples; in particular of *Geulincx* in Belgium (1625–1669), and *Malebranche,* in France (1638–1715). The latter maintained that causality is an attribute of God alone. Even in sense perception it is not we who act, but God puts the knowledge of the object into our minds, on occasion merely of its presentation to our senses. The error is therefore called **" Occasionalism."** God also exhibits to us in Himself any ideas He grants us: " we see all things in God." This is **Ontologism,** so called because it pretends that we get our ideas directly from things (ὄντα) existing in God and presented to our minds.

Article II.　Confusion Consequent on Cartesianism.

75. *Baruch Spinoza* (1632–1677) was the father of modern *Pantheism,* or *Monism,* that is, belief in the existence of only one substance. Born at Amsterdam of Jewish parents, he was excommunicated by the Synagogue for errors of doctrine. At the Hague he led a retired scholarly life, supporting himself by polishing lenses, while he corresponded with the most learned men of Europe. His entire system is founded on a mistaken definition of *substance,* as a thing which exists *in se,* in itself, and is conceived *per se,* that is, which, in order to be conceived, does not need a prior conception of anything else. He calls it *self-caused,* which is a contradiction in terms. He concludes from this wrong definition

that God is the only substance, for only one being can be self-existent; all other things are only determinations of God; they are God limited. This doctrine makes all men to be God, and therefore incapable of doing wrong; it destroys all morality, all law, all duty.

76. *John Locke* (1632–1704) has influenced thought in English-speaking countries to a remarkable extent. His style is excellent, his character was upright, he sincerely aimed at undoing some of the harm caused by Descartes, and he did refute his theory of innate ideas triumphantly; but at the same time he fell into serious errors, and unwittingly led his countrymen astray from **true** philosophy.

For, after proving that we have no inborn ideas, he leaves us no knowledge but what the senses can grasp and what the mind can observe in itself; now the senses can grasp only material accidents, and the mind only what the senses bring into it, and its own acts, which are also accidents; therefore he admits no real knowledge of *substance*. He defines substance as merely the complex idea of that which upholds and supports the simple ideas of color, taste, etc. The senses do not take in anything *universal;* therefore he admits no universal ideas, but teaches *Nominalism*. He also distinguishes nominal from real essences; we know the *nominal essences*, he says; that is, the complex ideas of color, sound, weight, etc., of bodies; but we do not know their real essence, that is, the inmost nature of any of them, for instance of a man, a brute, a plant, etc. Another leading error is his confusion of *ideas* with *phantasms;* for he says that the senses bring ideas into the passive mind. This error has become traditional in English philosophy, and it is to-

day at the root of various false systems of psychology
and epistemology.

His premises logically lead to materialism; but his
common sense made him refuse to draw such consequences. He is justly called the father of modern
Sensism; for, instead of innate ideas, which Descartes
had taught, he gives us only sense knowledge. In morals he made self-interest and the good of the many the
norm of right; in politics he wisely exalts the people
above the ruler; for the ruler is for the benefit of the
people, not the reverse.

77. Once **the nature of morality** had begun to be discussed, a large variety of novel theories on this matter
was put forth by English writers, and from England imported into France. The principal of these were the
following:

1. *Lord Shaftesbury* (1671–1713) makes the norm of
right and wrong consist in an innate esthetic sentiment,
by which we perceive the proper balance of our selfish
and our social impulses.

2. *Bernard Mandeville* (1670–1733) argues that private
vices are public benefits; for the excessive desire of food
and drink, the passions of ambition, envy, impatience,
etc., lead to labor, civilization, social life, etc. This theory was indignantly assailed by many; but it has prevailed in the teachings of Hutcheson, Butler, Adam
Smith and others.

3. *Francis Hutcheson* (1694–1747) claims that we have
a moral sense of what is beneficial for others and a natural love of the same. This sense acts in us as instinct
does in animals; it is God's provision to make men seek
the good of others as well as their own.

4. *Joseph Butler* (1692-1752) claims that the rule of right and wrong in us is our "conscience." Conscience, however, in his theory is not a deduction of practical reason, but a peculiar faculty directly approving and disapproving right and wrong acts.

5. *Adam Smith* (1723-1790) the celebrated author of "The Wealth of Nations," and the father of *Political Economy*, makes "sympathy" the rule of morality, calling an action good if it can elicit the sympathy of the spectators.

These English moralists, though theoretically destroying all true morality, produced no very deep impression on the British nation. But the poison of their empirical doctrines, when carried into France by Voltaire and Montesquieu, developed into rank materialism, hedonism and atheism, thus preparing the way for the French Revolution and the Reign of Terror.

78. **France,** too, originated some novel theories. 1. *The Abbé Condillac* (1715-1780) taught absolute *Sensism;* for he denied all knowledge except that of sensation. To explain how man gradually acquires knowledge, he imagines a statue which is first endowed with the sense of smell, and gradually with the other senses, last of all with the sense of touch. At first the statue experiences only pleasant and unpleasant feelings of various kinds, till the touch gives exernality to its perceptions. It is only by his superior sense of touch that man is above the brute. The good is the pleasing, evil that which displeases. Such false suppositions must of course lead to false conclusions.

2. *Helvétius* (1694-1771) puts self-interest as man's only motive of action. All differences among men arise from differences of education.

3. *Voltaire* (1694–1771) in his "Dictionaire Philosophic Portatif" spread broadcast all kinds of superficial and false ideas for the express purpose of destroying Christianity. He was no atheist, but a bitter hater of the Church. His main strength lay in his boldness, superficiality and effective style, seasoned with keen sarcasm.

4. *The Encyclopedia,* or "Dictionaire Raisonné des Arts, des Sciences et des Métiers," published from 1751 to 1772, promoted the same purpose. It was sceptical, designedly irreverent and brilliant with keen wit and caustic satire. Diderot, d'Alembert, Voltaire, Holbach and Rousseau were its principal authors.

5. *La Mettrie* (1709–1751) identifies the soul with the brain, the perfection of which constitutes man's superiority over the brute.

6. *Cabanis* (1757–1808) makes thought a mere secretion of the brain.

7. *Jean Jacques Rousseau* (1712–1778) advocates a return to the primitive state of nature, the savage state; he teaches that all authority is from the people through the social contract, and he would reform all education to suit such theories.

All these false teachings demoralized the French people, and ultimately brought about the Reign of Terror. Napoleon restored order by main force and able legislation; but he did not restore sound thought. Hence the atheism that has ever since been corroding religion and morality in France.

ARTICLE III. THE IDEALISTIC MOVEMENT.

79. 1. *Leibnitz* (1648–1716) was one of the greatest geniuses of modern times; he invented Calculus and the prin-

ciple of preëstablished harmony, the law of continuity,
etc. We mean by **the law of continuity** that, among all
existing beings in the universe, there is a gradual ascent
from the meanest to the noblest without a break in the
series. He defines *substance* as an independent power
of action. The universe consists of *monads*, or ultimate
elements; every one of which is a substance indivisible
and indestructible. Each monad reflects all the other
monads, consciously in spirits, unconsciously in mere
matter, and perfectly in the one grand monad, God.
God has so arranged all the monads that they act im-
manently, or within themselves, in a **preëstablished harmony.** The only proof of all this is that so it is best,
and God always does what is best. Ideas are worked
out in every soul, which are not derived from outward
objects; yet they are true, because they are in harmony
with their objects. The whole system is merely *a priori*,
a fancy structure.

2. *George Berkeley* (1685–1753), a Protestant bishop
of Cloyne, in Ireland, taught that we know ideas only,
not things; for all that we call qualities of matter de-
pends on the mind, which groups various subjective experiences, and attributes to them objective being. They
exist only in our mind: *esse est percipi*, that is, "the only
being of things is their being perceived." Yet all these
phenomena are orderly, constituting a cosmos, not a
chaos; for God produces them in our minds. There exist
only spirits, not bodies.

3. *David Hume* (1711–1776) drew the ultimate conclusions from Descartes's and Locke's false principles by
reducing all knowledge to **mere phenomenalism,** denying
our certainty with regard to the existence of either body

or mind.   In his "Treatise on Human Nature" he lays down the principle that our knowledge cannot reach beyond our experience.   In his "Enquiry Concerning Human Understanding" he maintains that we have no experience except of mental states, not even of the substantiality of our minds.   Nor do we know *causality*, but only the constant relation of succession, as of the Sun shining and crops growing.   We naturally expect that things formerly conjoined will always be so; but we have no right to expect this if there is no causality.   The logical outcome is **scepticism,** and metaphysics becomes an idle dream.

All subsequent systems of what is called Modern Philosophy are only efforts more or less original to correct glaring defects in preceding systems, or attempted substitutes for them.

CHAPTER III.

FROM KANT TO OUR OWN TIME.

FROM 1780 TO 1909.

80. The current of philosophic thought, after Latin had ceased to be the common language, became divided among the nations; philosophy itself became nationalized.

ARTICLE I. GERMAN PHILOSOPHY.

Immanuel Kant (1734–1804) had been captivated for a while by Hume's phenomenalism, when his mind rebelled against it for several reasons, in particular because the science of mathematics is evidently not a mere collection of phenomena. On the other hand he was unwilling to admit definite teachings, which he called *dogmas*, such as the existence of God, that of the soul, etc., and even the veracity of our faculties. He undertook, therefore, to make a critical examination of all our knowledge, which he styled **"A Critique of the Pure Reason."** By a critique Kant means an attempted scrutiny of the range and validity of our knowledge. Dogmatism, he says, assumes the reliability of our faculties, scepticism rejects it, he pretends to examine it. But at bottom he must admit or deny it; he really denies it.

He begins by teaching that our mind has receptivity

of *sensations,* which come to it from our internal and our external senses. These produce in the mind representations, which he calls *intuitions.* The mind combines the various intuitions which come to it from an object, say from an apple, forming thus by its spontaneity the *idea* of an apple.

It locates all its intuitions in *time* and *space.* Kant maintains that this location proceeds from the mind alone; time and space are *a priori* forms which we impose upon nature and do not derive from nature. He writes: "It sounds strange at first, but it is none the less certain, that the mind does not derive its own primitive cognitions from nature, but imposes them upon nature." Kant thought that this discovery of time and space as *a priori* forms of thought was the death knell, the *Mane, Thekel, Phares,* of dogmatism, while it is one of his own many dogmas. His admirer Weber exclaims: "Such is the immortal discovery of Kant, and one of the capital doctrines of Critical philosophy."

That capital doctrine is a capital error. And yet it is Kant's main proof to show that we do not know things as they are in themselves, the *noumena,* but only as they appear to us, the phenomena. Now, no man can seriously convince himself that time and space do not belong to things themselves but only to our view of them. Why have we locomotives if things are not distant from one another but only in our mind? But such distance is space; for *real space* is the relation between existing bodies. Our mind may imagine space to be limitless, and such limitless space has no real being out of the mind, but real space has. As to time, it is the measure of succession in things that change; and certainly things change successively.

81. As Kant makes the mind impose *a priori* forms on our sensations, so he makes it impose *a priori* forms on our judgments. According to him we judge one thing to be a *cause* and another an *effect,* not because they are so, but because it is our nature to judge them so. Thus, too, we judge one thing to be possible and another impossible, one thing necessary and another contingent, one a substance and another an accident, though they may not be such in themselves. These modes of judgments he calls *categories,* of which he assigns twelve, thus giving a new meaning to the ancient term category. But we cannot here explain the entire structure of his complicated edifice.

We must, however, notice another of his capital errors, that regarding his **synthetic judgments a priori.** A judgment is *analytic* when the meaning of the subject and the predicate shows by the mere analysis of both that they agree or disagree with one another; as: "the infinitely perfect being is good," for goodness is a perfection. The judgment is *synthetic* when the subject and predicate are brought together in some other way. This other way can only be experience or reasoning on what has been observed or experienced, and therefore the judgment is said to be *a posteriori,* posterior to experience; but Kant speaks of judgments which are neither analytical nor *a posteriori.* These come then from the mind itself, says Kant, not because the mind sees the agreement of the subject and predicate, but simply because it is the nature of the mind to impose its view upon the matter. For instance, "everything must have a reason for being," "two things equal to a third are equal to each other," etc.

Now all these are *a priori* judgments, necessarily and objectively true, and seen by the mind to be true on the careful consideration of the full meaning of the subjects and the predicates; *all a priori judgments are analytic.* When Kant refuses to admit the truth of such judgments in the objective reality, he destroys the science of mathematics and every other science, philosophy included. For all the sciences rest on the value of logical reasoning; and there is no value in reasoning if the principle is doubted which underlies the syllogism, namely: two things equal to a third are equal to each other. Kant's philosophy is suicidal.

To prove that pure reasoning is incapable of giving us true knowledge, Kant pretends to point out four **antinomies,** that is, four sets of contradictory judgments which are true while contradictory. These judgments are: 1. The antinomy of *quantity :* the world is limited in space and time, and yet it is unlimited in space and time; he attempts to prove both. 2. The antinomy of *quality :* matter is infinitely divisible and not infinitely divisible. 3. The antinomy of *relation :* there is liberty of choice and there is no liberty of choice. 4. The antinomy of *modality :* there must be a necessary being, and there need be no necessary being. These are four notorious quibbles; but Kant strives to make them appear respectable, and by them to destroy all objective certainty. With similar quibbles he attacks the existence of God, that of the soul, etc.

82. But Kant's **Criticism of the Practical Reason** tries to build up again what his other Criticism had pulled down. In this second work he discusses the question "What must I do?" and he answers: "I must act ac-

cording to a maxim which would admit of being regarded as a general law for all acting beings." He feels within him an imperative dictate which says, "I ought to do so or so." This is a *categorical imperative*, absolute, not conditional. The will of man imposes this rule on itself; and therefore our morality is *autonomous*, self-imposed. It is an independent morality, not even dependent on God. Kant fails to see that it is not our will that imposes this rule on itself; it is our understanding that makes known to us the duty of keeping the right order of things in our conduct. The rule of our reason comes from the Author of our being; it is the law of God.

From the fact that we must obey a law Kant draws three important conclusions: 1, That *we are free* agents; for only free agents are subject to a moral law. 2, That *our soul is immortal;* for compliance with duty improves us, and we are always capable of more and more improvement, so that we cannot reach our term in this life. Besides, sanctity is not attainable in this world; therefore there must be a future world. 3, Duty well performed deserves happiness; now, we cannot attain happiness in the next world without a good God; therefore *there is a good God.*

A third portion of Kant's critical study is the **"Critique of the Judgment."** It considers things as concordant among themselves or as fit for an end intended. Things concordant regard *the esthetic judgment;* they are the *beautiful* and the *sublime.* The beautiful pleases us because we feel we can unify the multiform; the sublime awes us because we feel we cannot do so. Things fit for a purpose regard *the teleological judgment.*

Kant had undertaken to refute Hume's phenomenal-

ism; but he failed to do so. He left philosophy in a
worse condition than he had found it; and he had opened
up regions of novel speculations and doubts, which have
employed the wits of numerous followers till the present
day.

83. Kant had accepted the existence of the material
world, and explained how the human mind fashions it to
suit our mental faculties; his system contained a dualism, mind and matter. **John Gottlieb Fichte** (1762 to
1814) attempted to put unity into Kantism, by making
all our knowledge merely subjective, denying the objective reality of sensations. The mind, the *Ego*, alone
exists; it thinks out the universe. Then, reflecting on its
thought, it distinguishes between itself and its mental
creations, self and not-self, subject and object; it calls
the subjective *thought*, the objective it calls *sensation*.
Thus the duality of spirit and matter is removed; for the
matter is nothing else than the thought of the spirit,
which posits itself and all else.

As Kant had added a practical portion to his speculations, and thus tried to undo some of the harm which
his "Critique of Pure Reason" had caused, so likewise
Fichte added a Practical System, which was intended to
effect the same benign purpose. But the two can
scarcely be considered as concordant parts of a whole
theory. In later life especially he emphasized the practical portion, particularly in an "Address to the German
Nation." His practical maxim is: "*Act according to thy
conscience*"; this precept regulates man's interior. The
other maxim regulates his exterior conduct: "*So limit
thy freedom that others may be free along with thee.*" When
this last principle is violated, then the State must inter-

fere. Besides, man must be religious; and religion adds to morality peace and life and blessed love.

84. Frederick William Joseph Schelling (1775 to 1854) was first a disciple of Fichte, but gradually changed his views and taught successively five different systems. A main feature of his shifting structure is the *absolute identity* of the subject knowing and the object known. He does not admit an *Ego* and a *non-Ego*, but only a *transcendental unity* of being and knowledge, of matter and spirit. For he argues thus: truth requires conformity between the subject knowing and the object known; but there can be no conformity without identity. This absolute identity, or the *Absolute's Indifference* to be one thing or another, is the center of all science, as well as of all existence; and the immediate perception, or pure intuition, of reason is the only organ or means by which man can come to the fountain of all truth.

The Absolute Identity itself is *God;* all *things* are only various modes of the existence of God. Next Schelling considers various things, matter and spirit, good and evil, life and non-life, etc., and sets forth how everything is a mode of the *Absolute Indifference;* the world is an epic poem without beginning and without end. His system is the poetry of an enthusiastic imagination ever speculating on new possibilities; but it is poetry, not philosophy. The theory has charmed many by its apparent combination of unity and variety; but it is a structure without foundation to its theory, and in practice destructive of morality. For it takes away all law and denies all liberty, without which two elements there can be no morality.

85. George William Frederick Hegel (1770 to 1831)

has had a large following, but his disciples interpret him
very diversely. For his great obscurity allows every
one to put his own meaning into his system. He maintained that pure conception in itself, and pure conception
alone, is true being; also that every thing rational is real,
and that every thing real is rational. He also makes
the beautiful, and God Himself, only mental phenomena.

With all this he is so obscure that many consider him
as a firm prop of Church and State, and his doctrines as
a perfect system of rational science. Some Hegelians as-
sert the personality of God; others deny it, except in as
far as God becomes self-conscious in human reason.
This latter view is real pantheism, and, if not taught by
Hegel, it follows at least from his principles.

But Hegel's pantheism is unlike Spinoza's; for the latter makes the Absolute an infinite substance, while Hegel's makes it an *infinite activity*, which becomes successively nature and spirit, so that nature and spirit are
mere manifestations of the Absolute. Hegel's is a philosophy of development, of which it notes three stages,
namely, the being *in-itself*, *out-of-self*, and *for-itself;* that
is, being, or thought, realizes itself by going out from
itself and returning to itself.

To put the right value on Hegel's system, we must consider what he undertakes to explain. Kant had failed
to put unity into his theory; Fichte gave it unity by
merging the object, the *thing-in-itself*, in the activity of
the subject, the *Ego;* Schelling merged subject and object in the indifference of the Absolute; Hegel substi-
tuted for the Absolute of indifference an Absolute of im-
manent activity. Hegel's Absolute is a process which

does not give forth matter and spirit, but becomes matter and spirit.

But we must bear in mind that in this whole theory the very purpose of philosophy is lost sight of. For the purpose of philosophy is the pursuit of truth, not of fiction; the conformity of our mind to the objects of knowledge: the world, the soul, the First Cause of all things— not the weaving of subjective theories, however ingenious and complete they may be, and how perfect in their unity and variety.

86. **John Frederick Herbart** (1776 to 1841) opposed the whole Hegelian system. He rightly maintained that the problem set for philosophy is not to construct a universe, but to accept the universe as it exists, and to explain it properly. He called his system **Realism,** giving a novel meaning to this term; for the old meaning was a counter-distinction to Nominalism and Conceptualism (n. 56) as regarding universals; but Herbart's Realism is opposed to Fichte's Idealism (n. 83), which denied the reality of the world of sense. Yet in the world of sense Herbart admits only the phenomenal. For he reasons thus: being admits of neither limitation nor negation; but all things in nature are limited; therefore they are not real, but merely phenomenal. And again: a thing cannot be one and yet many; but all things around us are one and many—for instance, a man is extension, movement, substance and accidents, etc.—therefore they are not real things.

Herbart is chiefly known in the United States on account of the application he made of philosophy to education. He was led to this by his acquaintance with Pestalozzi, the founder of a modern school of *Pedagogy.*

This makes it all the more regretable that he has fallen into many grievous errors; for false principles cannot be safe guides in the training of the child, especially when they concern the very nature of those faculties which are to be trained. Now Herbart does not even admit free-will in the child; for he teaches that the human will is nothing but thought, will is only the supremacy of the strongest idea.

87. **Arthur Schopenhauer** (1788 to 1860) attempts to defend and improve Kantism, seeking light for this purpose in Platonism and Buddhism. He admits in our knowledge a subject and an object, yet so that there is no object without a subject which posits it. But it is not the intellect but the will of the subject which posits it; the will is the noumenal cause of the phenomenon. Therefore his principal work is entitled "The World as Will and Representation."

By the *will* he means the natural impulse to live; it is common to vegetable, animal and human beings. It is a combative impulse tending to struggle for existence; and even in man it is not spiritual but merely brain action.

The subject is prompted to act by experiencing pain, pleasure being only a cessation of pain; positive pleasure is an illusion. He writes: "The simple truth is that we ought to be miserable, and so we are. The chief source of the serious evils which affect man is man himself: *homo homini lupus.* Whoever keeps this fact clearly in view beholds the world as a hell which surpasses that of Dante in this respect that one man must be the devil of another. . . . Life is a path of red-hot coals with a few cool places here and there."

We must individually strive to escape from pain: (*a*) By art, chiefly music, which lulls our conscious life. (*b*) By sympathy, which makes the sufferings of others our own, and thus substitutes the will-to-let-live for the will-to-live. (*c*) By negation of the will-to-live, whether by Christian asceticism or pagan Buddhism, the Nirvana of the philosopher. His theory, therefore, is a mixture of pantheism and pessimism.

ARTICLE II.   SCOTTISH PHILOSOPHY.

88. After Hume had carried the false principles of Descartes to their logical consequences, and left nothing but phenomenalism and scepticism to his followers in England and Scotland (n. 79, 3), a salutary reaction against his influence arose in his own country under the guidance of *Carmichael* and *Hutcheson*, but especially of *Reid*.

1. **Thomas Reid** (1710–1796), in his "Essays on the Powers of the Human Mind," proposed a system which he called *the Philosophy of Common Sense;* it has been distinctively designated as "the Scottish Philosophy." Discarding theories and hypotheses, he insists on our thorough conviction that we perceive bodies directly, as the common sense of all men declares. He accepts this belief as a foundation of certainty that must not be discussed, because it is an instinct of human nature. Yet an instinct not critically examined is only a blind impulse, and cannot be the foundation of rational knowledge. While thus wanting in the last analysis, his system provides for men a safe rule of action, and secures them from wandering far astray. It is no deep philosophy, nor is its foundation solid; but it is practically safe.

2. **Dugald Stuart** (1753–1828), a disciple of Reid, expounded his master's teachings in works of elegant taste and varied learning, thus popularizing the study of philosophy and extending the influence of Reid's system. Besides, he greatly improved on the theory by referring the judgment of right and wrong to reason and not to a moral sense, as Reid had done.

3. **Sir William Hamilton** (1788–1856) is far from being equally sound. He supposed that the task of philosophy was to consider the conditions of knowledge. This is done by the study of the mind, by psychology, which he called metaphysics. The mind knows only phenomena, he teaches, and he adds: "Our whole knowledge of mind and matter is thus only relative; of existence, absolute and in itself, we know nothing." By his erudition and scholarship Hamilton secured a large following. But his *relativity of knowledge* was both obscure and untrue; it prepared the way for agnosticism.

4. **Henry Longueville Mansel** (1820–1871) concluded from the relativity of natural knowledge the necessity of revelation, and therefore of faith which accepts revelation.

Article III.   French Philosophy.

89. We have seen (n. 78) that Condillac, Helvétius, Voltaire, etc., had ruined all philosophy in France; and the Reign of Terror which soon followed had destroyed all pretense of public virtue. This situation led the royalist **De Bonald** (1754–1840) into novel speculations to save morality and religion. He maintained that human reason is powerless to attain to truth, that man could not have acquired any ideas but through language;

therefore that all our knowledge, both of words and of things, must have come to our race by revelation of the Creator. Together with language God must have given us the principal truths of religion, and also the principles of the metaphysical, moral and political order. Thus he rests all certainty, not on evidence, but on revelation.

About the same time, and partly for the same reasons, the Abbé **De Lamennais** (1782–1854), after zealously defending the Church for a dozen years with distinguished ability, and at first with conspicuous success, undertook in 1830 to start the newspaper *l'Avenir* for the purpose of advocating the union of the Church with popular liberty, together with the abolition of royalty, of the nobility and of the Concordat. When these novel and revolutionary doctrines were condemned at Rome, he refused to submit, and soon began an open warfare against the Church.

Before his apostasy he had written his " Essay on Indifference," in which he taught the system of **Traditionalism.** The worship of Reason, which, in the person of a degraded woman, had been enthroned on the altar of the cathedral of Paris, had discredited human reason in the eyes of the most religious people. Hence De Lamennais was led to maintain that the light of human knowledge cannot have come to man by reason but only by revelation; tradition has handed that knowledge down to us, embodied in the collective thought, or universal consent of mankind.

In his later work, " A Sketch of a Philosophy," he adds elements of mysticism, rationalism and pantheism. The Traditionalism which he had so vigorously advocated, was defended by many well-meaning men as a reaction against rationalism; but, instead of benefiting the faith as they had hoped it would do, it rather led to scepticism.

90. Meanwhile **Victor Cousin** (1792–1867), by his brilliant lectures in Paris and his numerous and scholarly writings, attracted the favorable attention of Europe to his views on the history of philosophy, and to his own peculiar system of **Eclecticism.** He divided all systems of philosophy into four classes, namely: sensism, idealism, scepticism and mysticism. It is the part of common sense, he claimed, to gather the elements of truth scattered through those various speculations. In his effort to do so, he followed the inductive process, which he applied to the facts of consciousness.

He thus finds within himself first the *will power*, which he considers as the characteristic of personality, and secondly, *facts of sensation* and *acts of reason.* In our will we perceive *causality*, a fact which many theorizers have failed to recognize; our reason reveals the finite, the infinite and the relations between them. Thus psychology enables us to reason from contingent things to the Absolute Cause, the Absolute Substance, etc., in fact, to all the great truths of life. Cousin had begun with the spirit of a rationalist; gradually he elaborated his own system of **Spiritualism,** as he wished his theory to be called. He went further, and suggested at least that his reasoning led up to the porch of Divine revelation.

91. **Auguste Comte** (1798–1857) is the author of what is called **Positivism.** This system teaches that man cannot know anything but positive facts which fall under the senses, together with the relations which the mind can trace between these facts. Every sensible man accepts such facts as real; why, then, are Comtists alone

called Positivists? Because of their denial that we can know anything else. They should, therefore, properly be called "Negativists." Comte of course denies, in keeping with his main teachings, that we can know anything about God, the soul, a future life, etc. He also maintains that our knowledge is only relative, because it is derived from the relations between things.

In early times, he says, men considered all events as coming from the voluntary action of the gods—it was the *theological* age; in the *metaphysical* age men traced events to occult and abstract forces; now, in the *positive* age, we merely state facts. Laws or theories are mere abstractions, not causes. He also attempted to make Positivism into a religion, which would be the direct worship of "Humanity."

Comte has had a large following in English-speaking countries, rather than in France. He did not deal in metaphysical speculations, but in the physical and social sciences. In fact, his views would make metaphysics impossible; for the latter science is incompatible with Positivism, which excludes the knowledge of whatever is beyond sensation.

Henry Count of St. Simon (1760–1835) did not elaborate a system, but he sowed the seed of social changes which his disciples developed into the system of **Industrialism**; and with this his name has become historically connected. With this plan is combined the theory of perpetual progress, or **Social Evolution,** which strives to establish on earth an era of temporal happiness for all, irrespective of religion and the future life.

Article IV.   English Philosophy.

92. A large number of English writers have during the last two centuries proposed and propagated various false theories.

1. **Joseph Priestley** (1733–1804) was an eminent chemist, who, like many other scientists, was incapable of any wider views than those belonging to his specialty. He made thought a mere function of the brain, thus promoting rank materialism.

2. **Erasmus Darwin** (1731–1802) explained ideas as being mere motions, contractions and other modifications of those nerves which are connected with the organs of sense. All further mental actions are referred to the association of such ideas.

3. **Jeremy Bentham** (1748–1832) made the purpose of morality to consist in the greatest happiness to the greatest number; we must seek pleasure, yet not as egoists only, but also as altruists.

4. **James Mill** (1773–1836) wrote "The Analysis of the Phenomena of the Human Mind" to prove that our ideas are only the remnants of our sensations, and our beliefs are the inseparable associations of our ideas with one another. Morality is the utility of actions to increase happiness.

5. **John Stuart Mill** (1806–1873) a son of the preceding, composed a "System of Logic," which has been extensively taught in English and American colleges; but it is far from being a safe guide. He rejects all *a priori* knowledge, and makes experience the sole source of certainty. It follows from his principles that even a circle may not, for all we know, be round in other planets, for

we have not been there to see circles; nor may a triangle
there have three sides; axioms are only generalizations
of our experiences; causation is but invariable sequence;
our aim should ever be to procure the greatest happiness
for all sentient beings. He has, however, benefited Logic by formulating good rules for experimental investi-
gations.

93. **The philosophy of Evolution** has held the field of
speculation for the last eighty years, not in England
only, but in all civilized lands. Evolution, in its widest
meaning, may be *defined* as the process of formation of
more complex from simpler forms of beings, the passage
of the homogeneous into the heterogeneous. In a nar-
rower meaning, it signifies the formation of more perfect
from less perfect *species* of organisms. In this latter
signification Evolution had been spoken of, as we have
seen (n. 15), by so early a philosopher as Anaximander;
Aristotle, St. Augustine, Leibnitz and others had sus-
pected its action in the world.

We cannot prove to a demonstration that it has ever
taken place; but very many modern scientists scarcely
allow its former existence to be questioned. They consider the material world to have been evolved into its
present state from a mere nebula of world stuff. Religion has no quarrel with Evolution as such, but only with
infidel Evolution. Ecclesiastes says: "I have seen the
trouble which God hath given to the sons of men to
be exercised in it. He hath made all things good in
their time, and hath delivered the world to their consideration, so that man cannot find out the work which
God hath made from the beginning to the end"
(III, 10, 11).

94. The principal philosophers who have written on Evolution are the following:

1. **Charles Darwin** (1809–1883) conceived an ingenious explanation of supposed processes by which a few simple and primitive organisms may have been gradually, through countless ages, evolved into all the species of plants and animals that now exist or ever have existed on earth. He ascribes such changes to natural tendencies in organisms to vary their progeny, and to transmit such *variations* by *heredity* from generation to generation. In *the struggle for existence* that would often occur, he traced the natural *survival of the fittest*, and invented laws of *natural* and *sexual selection*, which, he thought, would tend to produce ever more perfect organisms, ultimately man himself.

He does not attempt to show how the first plants and animals originated; in the series of successive developments he admits there are numerous gaps which he cannot bridge over; and in his "Descent of Man" he utterly fails to prove that the human soul was evolved from matter, a change which is metaphysically impossible. In all his theory he makes the mistake of supposing that the marvelous order conspicuous in the universe can have resulted from blind forces, not especially provided for the purpose by the wise Creator, and that whatever can be imagined to have happened has actually occurred.

2. **Alfred Russel Wallace** (born 1823) proposed the same theory as Darwin and at the same time as he; but he was less rash in his speculations, not including man in the series of evolutions, and admitting the directing wisdom of the Creator. His greater prudence made him less of a favorite with the many writers and readers who wel-

comed Darwinism as a plausible way out of the necessity of admitting a wise Creator.

3. **John Tyndall** (1829–1893), a distinguished physicist, in his notorious address at Belfast in 1874 as President of the British Association, shocked the public ear of England by his materialistic utterance that all the elements which made up a genius like Newton were contained in the nebula from which our planetary system was eventually evolved.

All the evolutionists so far mentioned were skilful scientists in some department or other, in which they rendered valuable services to their fellow-men. But they could not leave metaphysics and religion alone, which, however, lay beyond the grasp of most of them. They applied to what is beyond the physical such processes of investigation as suited their physical specialties. Such was especially the case with the following writer.

4. **Thomas H. Huxley** (1835–1895) made himself the principal spokesman of the infidel party of evolutionists. Deprecating the odium attached to the name *materialist*, and yet unwilling to be classed with *spiritualists*, he assumed the title of **Agnostic**, pretending that no man can answer the great questions of life. He played a double part: when addressing the learned he spoke of Darwinism as a theory only; but to the laboring classes, in his "Origin of Species," "Man's Place in Nature" and "Lay Sermons," he taught the most materialistic features of Darwinism, and proclaimed explicitly that no other system of Evolution is possible. He spent a long, energetic and learned life in purposely teaching infidelity.

5. **Herbert Spencer** (1820–1903) had given definite form to the doctrine of Evolution as early as A.D. 1855,

four years before Darwin published his "Origin of Species." He was *the* philosopher of Evolution; he has even been called by his admirers the Aristotle of modern times. He made Evolution to apply, not merely to life and its forms on earth, but to the whole system of the universe. Relegating the beginning of things to the *unknowable,* he labored to show that all the conditions of the planetary system are due to alternations of evolutions and dissolutions. In his "Synthetic Philosophy" he undertook to embrace in one consistent exposition the workings of Evolution in biology, psychology, morality and sociology. As to the validity of our knowledge of bodies, we can only grasp "the unknown correlations of our feelings and the relations among our feelings."

Ethical truths and sentiments are thus accounted for: "the experiences of utility, organized and consolidated through all past generations of the human race have been producing corresponding nervous modifications, which, by continued transmission and accumulation have become in us certain faculties of moral intuitions— certain emotions corresponding to right and wrong conduct which have no apparent basis in the individual experiences of utility."

He did not live to complete his great work on "Synthetic Philosophy"; but he lived long enough to see and acknowledge its unsatisfactory nature, and some of his more important errors. Thus in his "Reflections," published a short time before his death, he admits that a purposeless universe seems worthless, that the consciousness evolved in every child suggests an omnipresent consciousness, that we must speculate as to the wherefore of the process out of which the worlds and their lives have come; whereas in his earlier work on "First Principles" he had considered religion as a mere sentiment.

6. **St. George Mivart** (1827–1900) also wrote in defense of Evolution, refuting in his "Genesis of Species" the atheistic interpretation of this process, and in his learned work "Truth" explaining the Scholastic philosophy of knowledge, and showing it to be in accord with the teachings of physical science. The peculiar process of Evolution which he suggests may or may not be the true one; but he certainly treats it with deep knowledge of sound principles.

John Henry Newman (1801–1890) first, while yet an Anglican, the principal leader of the Oxford movement, which led large numbers of learned clergymen and laymen with him into the Catholic Church, and later in life honored with the dignity of Cardinal, was one of the most philosophic writers of the nineteenth century. Though most of his discourses and writings dealt directly with religious subjects, he generally viewed the matters treated from the standpoint of reason as well as from that of revelation. He examined all doctrines and arguments with a peculiarly keen analytic mind, tracing conclusions to their first principles, whether these were of the natural or of the supernatural order. But his most obvious title to rank among philosophers is his "Grammar of Assent," in which he formally discusses the first principles of certainty as they affect the most important convictions of men.

Some of his views in that work are presented in a manner as original as it is convincing to the student. For instance, he insists much on the consideration that "our apprehension of a proposition varies in strength, and it is stronger when it is concerned with a proposition expressive to us of things than when concerned with a proposition expressive of notions"; because "what is concrete exerts a force and makes an impression on the mind which nothing abstract can rival" (p. 36). He valued more, in practical matters, including those of religion, the certainty arising from a number of converging probabilities than from a clear-cut syllogism.

In proving the existence of God he laid special stress on the testimony which conscience bears to the obligatory nature of the natural law. As the material universe leads the human intellect to seek and find a First Cause which is adequate to account for the facts, so the moral universe, which exists in the consciences of men, points to something above and beyond itself which the intellect pronounces to be the One Personal God.

This perfectly correct argument was misinterpreted by the Modernists, who wished to make Newman appear as an advocate of their doctrine of immanence. But the charge has been triumphantly refuted by the Most Rev. Bishop O'Dwyer of Limerick in his pamphlet entitled "Cardinal Newman and the Encyclical *Pascendi Dominici Gregis.*" Perhaps no writer during the nineteenth century exerted a stronger influence in behalf of truth in England than Cardinal Newman.

ARTICLE V. PHILOSOPHY IN AMERICA.

95. From colonial times speculations on philosophic matters have attracted the attention of many learned men in this country, though few Americans have built up systems of thought that have commanded general at-

tention. Since the people here were mostly religiously minded before the present system of public schools had become prevalent, philosophy among them often took the form of efforts to support their Church doctrines by reason; while on the other hand the spirit of liberty, so dominant in their political life, impelled not a few of their writers to drive false principles to their logical consequences. Several of the American philosophers merit special mention.

1. **Jonathan Edwards** (1703–1758) is one of the most conspicuous among them. He attempted to conciliate the Calvinistic theology with the principles of reason. In his "Treatise on the Will" he endeavored to prove that the Calvinistic notions of God's moral government are not contrary to the common sense of mankind. To effect this purpose he maintains that virtue does not consist in the will's *free* compliance with duty, in fact that the liberty of self-determination is an impossibility, since it would exclude God's foreknowledge of our free acts. He teaches that sin is the total inability of man to observe the Divine law. Edwards had undertaken an impossible task, but he labored at it with much ingenuity and devotedness.

2. **Jonathan Edwards Junior** (1745–1801), son of the preceding, was president of Union College. He adopted most of his father's teachings; and, besides, he elaborated what is called "The New England Theory of the Atonement," which has been widely adopted in this land.

3. **Samuel Johnson, D.D.** (1696–1790) published through Benjamin Franklin in 1752 his *Elementa Philosophica* a clear and able treatise, teaching mainly the doctrine of Malebranche (n. 74).

4. **Benjamin Franklin** (1706–1790), the renowned physicist and statesman, by his "Reflections of Poor Richard" gained deserved credit for great practical wisdom. He was most influential in exciting and directing mental activity among his fellow-citizens.

In his day the political relations of America with the freethinkers of France caused their writings to be eagerly read on this side of the Atlantic, and gained them many admirers. Hume also was then at the height of his fame, and Locke's "Essay on the Human Understanding" was the favorite text-book in American colleges. Thus a powerful impulse was given to philosophic speculations; and these were often of an injurious kind. But the Scottish school had also wide vogue in the United States, especially after the sad fruits of infidel teachings had begun to be realized.

5. **Thomas Upham** (1799–1867), professor in Bowdoin College, energetically opposed the spread of infidel notions by his able text-books inculcating the teachings of Dugald Stewart (n. 88), modified by his own reasonings.

6. **Orestes A. Brownson** (1803–1876), one of the deepest thinkers and ablest writers of the nineteenth century, published during twenty-five years *Brownson's Quarterly Review*, almost every article of which was from his own pen. An earnest convert to the Church, he has left a rich treasury of information for Catholic readers, the use of which has been made readily available by a judicious new edition in twenty volumes, supplemented with a detailed topical index by his son Col. Henry F. Brownson. This last named author gives the following analysis of his father's philosophy:

"Brownson always disclaimed having originated any

system of philosophy, and acknowledged freely whatever he borrowed from others; but he had worked out and arrived at substantially the philosophy of his later writings before he ever heard of Gioberti, from whom he obtained the formula *ens creat existentias,* which Gioberti expressed in the formula *ens creat existens,* to indicate the ideal or intelligible object of thought. By the analysis of thought he finds that it is composed of three separate elements—subject, object, and their relation, simultaneously given. Analysis of the object shows that it is likewise composed of three elements simultaneously given—the ideal, the empirical, and their relation. He distinguishes the ideal intuition, in which the activity is in the object presenting or offering itself, and empirical intuition or cognition, in which the subject as well as the object acts. Ideal intuition presents the object, reflection takes it as represented sensibly; that is, in case of the ideal, as represented in language. Identifying ideas with the categories of the philosophers, he reduced them to these three: Being, Existences, and their Relation. The necessary is Being; the contingent, Existences; and their Relation, the creative act of Being. Being is God, personal because He has intelligence and will. From Him as First Cause, proceed the physical laws; and as Final Cause, the moral laws, commanding to worship Him, naturally or supernaturally, in the way and manner He prescribes." (The Catholic Encyclopedia, Art. Brownson.)

7. **Waldo Emerson** (1803–1882) is popularly considered as a great philosopher, the founder of *Transcendentalism.* He was indeed a versatile genius, an impressive writer and lecturer, and remarkable for bold and novel

thoughts; he often sent forth, in prose and verse, such flashes of genius as kindled other minds, some of which gave a systematic form to his conceptions. But he was no systematic thinker; for he says of himself: "I do not know what argumentations are in reference to any expression of thought. I delight in telling what I think; but if you ask me how I dare say so, or why it is so, I am the most helpless of mortal men."

He often affirmed the existence of a transcendental faculty in man, an intuitive religion and perception of God. The preacher of religion should be, he maintained, "A new-born bard of the Holy Ghost, and should cast behind him all conformity (with any denomination), and acquaint men at first hand with the Deity." He believed in an Over-Soul as a light guiding men, the light of intuitive perception; he took God to be the soul of the world, and the soul of man one with such a God.

But originality and boldness of thought and expression do not make a philosopher; systematic thought is essential for all philosophy, and conformity of the thought to the objective truth for sound philosophy. In both these qualities Emerson's writings are very deficient. If he is mentioned here among philosophers, it is because of the opportunity thus afforded of exposing a popular and pernicious error regarding his reputation.

Emerson is also exalted by some as a model of English style; but his style is labored and unnatural, more remarkable for conceit than for ease and classic grace.

8. In the middle of the nineteenth century **Rev. C. S. Henry** published his "Moral and Philosophical Essays," and one of the best works on the "History of Philosophy" in English.

9. Among the soundest thinkers during the latter half of the nineteenth century in this country was the Scotchman **James McCosh,** president of Princeton College, New Jersey, the avowed and able critic of Hamilton and Kant, on the one hand, and of Mill and Herbert Spencer, on the other. He also published an effective "Defense of Fundamental Truths," and some thoughtful volumes on "Realism," that is, on the reality of our knowledge.

Dr. Friedrich Ueberweg, in his "History of Philosophy," Vol. II, gives a brief account of some sixty more philosophical writers in America during the nineteenth century. But none of them have founded a distinct school, or have had a numerous following. Their systems were the speculations of individuals, or repetitions of European theories. Those which were original resembled dissolving views, none of which held the attention of the learned long enough to make a lasting impression.

Article VI. Italian and Spanish Philosophy.

96. The principal Italian philosophers during the last two centuries:

1. **Roger Boscovich, S. J.** (1711–1787), professor at the Roman College, was the founder of the system of **Dynamism.** This system makes matter consist of simple ultimate elements, or monads, endowed with two distinct powers: one of these keeps the monads at a distance from one another, thus giving extension to bodies; the other attracts them towards one another, thus giving solidity to bodies. Leibnitz also had made the material universe consist of ultimate monads (n. 79); but he had gratuitously attributed to the monads such fanciful and

extravagant natures as deprived his theory of all plaus-
ibility. Boscovich confined himself to a far more modest scheme; though he, too, was unable to demonstrate its
objective reality, and failed to give satisfactory answers
to some strong objections against it.

2. **Paschale Galuppi** (1770–1846), the chief representative in Italy of the **Critical** school, attempted to vindi-
cate the validity of our intellectual knowledge against
the sensism of Locke and Condillac, the subjective categories of Kant, and Reid's arbitrary admission of common sense judgments. He also proved that Kant's synthetic judgments *a priori* are really analytical judgments,
in which the attribute is contained in the subject. General ideas come from comparison and abstraction. But
with all this he rested his system too much on a subjective foundation, which failed to support the objective
truth of our knowledge. In his practical philosophy he
is generally in accord with the Scholastics.

3. **Antonio Rosmini-Serbati** (1797–1855), a priest of
most saintly life, at one time minister of instruction in
the cabinet of Pius IX, the founder also of the learned
and pious "Institute of Charity," originated the Italian
school of **Idealism.** He reduces the problem of our
knowledge to an intellectual perception of reality. The
reality perceived by every mind is simple, one, universal
and necessary, it is the very intelligence of God, perma-
nently communicated to the human mind under the
form of pure ideality. All transcendental ideas, logical
principles, substance, causality, etc., are potentially contained in it, and become distinct through the process of
reflection. Our universal ideas are but subjective determinations of the infinite ideality.

Rosmini also teaches that chemical atoms possess a principle of life, that there is a universal soul in nature, which, however, is individualized in the countless beings of the universe. Spontaneous generation is a natural consequence. His practical philosophy led him to advocate radical measures with regard to Church and State, in particular concerning education. When some of his writings were in consequence placed on the *Index Expurgatorius*, his docility on the occasion proved that his personal virtue far exceeded the wisdom of his philosophic speculations.

4. **Vincenzo Gioberti** (1801–1853), also a priest of peculiar views on theoretic and practical questions, traced out a special form of **Ontologism** as the only road to certain knowledge. Our mind, he maintained, has an immediate intuition of "God creating the world," *Ens creans existens*, but it requires reflection to realize the truth. This reflection is not merely the analysis of our mental acts, but also the consideration of the object intuited. The *Ens*, or *Being*, gives us ontology and theology; the copula *creating* originates the science of time and space—mathematics—and also the sciences of the true, the good and the beautiful—logic, ethics and esthetics; while the predicate *existens* originates the knowledge of spirit and matter—psychology, cosmology and the physical sciences. Since the object *Ens creans existens* reveals itself to our mind, our knowledge of it is necessarily well founded and certain. The whole system is but a castle in the air.

5. **Jaime L. Balmes** (1810–1848) a Spanish priest, a very prodigy of talent and industry, fulfilled in a brief space a career of uncommon usefulness in the field of philosophic thought. His work entitled "Protestant-

ism and Catholicity Compared in Their Effects on the Civilization of Europe" is a profound philosophy of the history of modern times; it is replete with sound thought and valuable erudition. His "Fundamental Philosophy" is an able exposition of the doctrine of St. Thomas, cast in a new mold to suit the intellectual condition of his own time. His "Elements of Philosophy" which soon became a favorite text-book in the schools of Spain, showed how his lofty genius deemed it a worthy task to guide the mind of youth. All these works, and also his "Criterion" and "The Art of Thinking," exist in English translations.

Before composing them he had thoroughly studied, not only the Scholastics, but also the leading modern philosophers; for he loved to discover and assimilate the scattered crumbs of wholesome thought found in this vast literature of varied speculations. He was thus led to admit a few opinions which cannot stand the test of thorough criticism. In particular the Catholic Encyclopedia remarks that "he perhaps accords too much to an intellectual instinct, a theory of the Scottish school (n. 88), and too little to objective evidence in the perception of truth. In psychology he rejects the *intellectus agens* (the abstractive intellect) and the *species intelligibilis* (intermediary representations), and he holds the principle of life in brutes to be naturally imperishable. These, however, are but accidental and relatively unimportant divergencies from the permanent body of traditional philosophy." (Art. Balmes.) His great merit lies in having presented the Scholastic system of thought in a new form and made it acceptable to the exacting intellect of his contemporaries.

97. **Neo-Scholasticism** is Scholasticism rejuvenated, restored to its original vigor, such as it possessed in the thirteenth century, when the genius of St. Thomas Aquinas had wedded the Peripatetic, or Aristotelian, philosophy to the doctrines of the Church of God. From this happy union of natural and supernatural truth had sprung a progeny of learned men, not indeed gifted with infallibility, actually dissenting from one another on many minor details, yet united on the great truths of life, who have perpetuated the system of the great schools, or universities, of the Middle Ages to the present day.

But Scholasticism had suffered from the human infirmities of old age. In its youth it had readily assimilated the productions of the natural sciences, such as it found them in the imperfect learning of those times. Of late those fruits have multiplied exceedingly, but little was done for some time to assimilate them into the enfeebled organism. The old system had also been surcharged with effete matter, which required to be purged away. It has now been rejuvenated and restored to its original vigor and clearness of sight. By taking into itself the fruits so copiously supplied by the physical sciences in modern times, Scholasticism is now growing to the full proportion of its manhood, and exhibiting to the eyes of the learned world a vast, strong and well-developed frame of theoretical and practical wisdom, one in its structure, yet manifold in its activity, permanent as the truth itself, yet adapting its action from day to day to the changing circumstances of its new surroundings.

98. An obvious **difference between medieval and modern Scholasticism** lies in the purpose chiefly aimed at by each. The medieval strove to bring into harmony the speculations of reason with the doctrines of revelation, so that knowledge should be reduced to unity in the human mind, and that nothing should be considered true in philosophy and yet false in theology, or the reverse. This task has long since been performed in its main outlines. But the purpose of Neo-Scholasticism is to adapt its principles to the state of modern science, as far as this state is conformable to the objective truth, and to rectify it where it is not correct.

For this purpose it is of the utmost importance that true science be carefully distinguished from such novel speculations as are not conformable to the truth of things. *Theories* are not science; they come and go; they must prove their conformity with truth before philosophy can be expected to square itself with them. But when a truth formerly unknown has been established by careful observation, philosophy must then consider it; such is the task set for Neo-Scholasticism.

Nor is the task always an easy one. Scholasticism is not throughout reason pure and simple; like the physical sciences, it also contains some theories not strictly demonstrated, for instance the theory of *matter and form,* which explains the constitution of bodies. Such theories must not be stubbornly defended, but tested by the facts of nature which modern sciences have made known to us; and the theories must be modified and even abandoned if proved to be at variance with facts.

99. But to do so wisely the Scholastic philosopher must know the facts of science; and, therefore, he must

make himself familiar with **the various sciences** which claim to make such discoveries. "The difficulty is indeed a serious one," writes Cardinal Mercier, a foremost leader of Neo-Scholasticism, " nor is it in the power of any individual to surmount it. Therefore it is that association must make up for the insufficiency of the isolated individual; that men of analysis and of synthesis must come together, and form, by their daily intercourse and united action, an atmosphere suited to the harmonious and equal development both of science and of philosophy." (Apud M. De Wulf, "Scholasticism Old and New," translated by Coffey, page 209.)

But it is not enough for Neo-Scholasticism to assimilate newly discovered truths; it must also refute **modern errors,** such especially as are deceiving the present generation. Such in particular are the subjective theories of Kant, Fichte, Hegel, Schelling, etc., the positivism of Comte, the agnosticism of Huxley and Spencer, etc.

100. **The Neo-Scholastic movement** had already made some progress when, in the year 1878, Pope Leo XIII, in his Encyclical *Inscrutabili Dei Providentia* commended its efforts, and soon after, in other weighty documents, traced the lines on which its study should be conducted. The principal source of progress in this new field is the "Philosophical Institute" of Louvain, Belgium, where the learned Professor, now Cardinal, Mercier and several able coöperators have, since 1880, cultivated biology, physics, chemistry, embryology, histology, physiology, psychophysiology and similar material sciences, in their connection with cosmology, psychology and other branches of metaphysics. (See Coffey's

translation of De Wulf, "Scholasticism Old and New,"
Appendix.)

101. While the Neo-Scholastics at Louvain have been
chiefly busied in observing the progress of the physical
sciences to which the old teaching is to be adapted, other
Catholic thinkers in various lands have been working on
restatements and readjustments of the ancient metaphysics, discarding from it useless questions, emphasizing
its most important teachings, and pointing out their
bearing upon the leading errors of modern thought. In
particular: 1. *Joseph Kleutgen, S. J.* (1811–1885), published the first complete course of Scholastic philosophy
in the German language. He displayed such ability in
this matter that, when Leo XIII began his great work
of reconstructing the teaching of philosophy and theology, he made Father Kleutgen prefect of studies of the
Gregorian University in Rome. The two most important works of this author are "Die Philosophie der Vorzeit" and "Die Theologie der Vorzeit," i.e., The Philosophy and the Theology of Former Ages. In the former
he gives a complete system of philosophy based on the
principles of the Scholastics. While not entering into
all the details commonly discussed in text-books of philosophy, and even avoiding the familiar mode of formal
theses and arguments, imitating on the contrary the
style and arrangement of modern writers, he discusses
the leading questions of criteriology, ontology, cosmology, psychology, and natural theology. All along he
strives chiefly to bring out the old doctrine in all its
beauty, and the solid arguments that support it in all
their strength.

In every tract he states the charges made against the

Scholastic doctrine, refutes them, shows the untenableness of the hypotheses proposed instead of the Scholastic theories, and compares the advantages secured by holding either the old or the new philosophic teachings.

In the "Theologie der Vorzeit " he compares the philosophical explanations of the doctrines of faith given by Catholic theologians who adhere to the so-called Modern philosophy with the explanations preferred by the Scholastics. Hence this work, too, is philosophic in its character; it discusses certain points not treated in the other.

2. In England the Jesuit Fathers have published a restatement of the Scholastic philosophy with adaptations to modern circumstances in their widely known "Stonyhurst Philosophical Series." It comprises the following volumes:

"Logic," by Richard F. Clarke, S. J., formerly professor in St. John's College, Oxford.

"First Principles of Knowledge," by John Rickaby, S. J.

"General Metaphysics," by the same author.

"Psychology," by Michael Maher, S. J., which in its enlarged edition is the ablest work on the subject in English. It is a masterpiece of Neo-Scholasticism.

"Natural Theology," by Bernard Boeder, S. J.

"Moral Philosophy" (Ethics and Natural Law), by Joseph Rickaby, S. J.

"Political Economy," by Charles Stanton Devas, Esq., M.A. Examiner in Political Economy at the Royal University, Ireland.

3. Besides the Stonyhurst Series, many able works written in the best spirit of Neo-Scholasticism have been published by *various English writers*. Thus the cele-

brated *Summa Contra Gentiles* of St. Thomas Aquinas has been translated into English, with learned notes and other adaptations to the modern mind, by Joseph Rickaby, S. J., with the title "God and His Creatures."

"The Metaphysics of the Schools" in three volumes, is a most learned contribution to philosophy from the pen of Thomas J. Harper, S. J.

St. George Mivart, the renowned scientist, has labored with distinguished success to show the agreement between Scholasticism and Modern Science in his books entitled "Truth" and "The Origin of Human Reason."

John Gerard, S. J., attacks the false pretences of modern scientists in his "Evolutionary Philosophy," "The Old Riddle and Its Newest Answer," "Science and Scientists," "Science and Romance."

William G. Ward has published "The Philosophy of Theism" in two volumes. Many articles written in the same spirit of the Neo-Scholastics have appeared in various Catholic periodicals, especially in *The Dublin Review*, *The American Catholic Quarterly Review*, and *The Month*, the organ of the Jesuits in England.

4. The restatement of the Scholastic teachings with adaptations to modern needs is not confined to works written in the living languages of the present day. Many *Latin works* have been published since the middle of last century which have the spirit, if not the name, of Neo-Scholastic philosophy. The following deserve special mention:

Dominicus Palmieri, S.J.—"Institutiones Philosophicæ," three volumes.

J. M. Cornoldi, S.J.—"Philosophia Speculativa," four volumes.

CARDINAL ZIGLIARA—"Summa Philosophica," three volumes.

CAJ. SANSEVERINO—"Elementa Philosophiæ Christianæ," three volumes.

G. LAHOUSSE, S. J.—"Prælectiones Logicæ et Metaphisicæ," four volumes.

THEOD. MEYER, S. J.—"Institutiones Juris Naturalis," two volumes.

TILMAN PESCH, S. J.—"Prælect. Philos. Schol. Brevis Conspectus," four volumes.

MATTH. LIBERATORE, S. J.—"Institutiones Philosophicæ," three volumes.

SALV. TONGIORGI, S. J.—"Institutiones Philosophicæ," three volumes.

A LIST OF

SELECT WORKS ON PHILOSOPHY.

I. ALL THE WORKS MENTIONED IN N. 101.

II. AQUINAS, ST. THOMAS—"Aquinas Ethicus," i.e., the moral teachings of St. Thomas translated and annotated by Joseph Rickaby, S. J.

AVELING—"The God of Philosophy."

AZARIAS, BRO.—"Aristotle and the Christian Church."

BALMES—"European Civilization," "Fundamental Philosophy," "Criterion."

BOWEN, FRANCIS—"Modern Philosophy from Descartes to Schopenhauer," often incorrect.

CATHREIN-GETTELMAN, S. J.—"Socialism."

CONWAY, JAS. J., S. J.—"Christian Ethics."

COPPENS, CHARLES, S. J.—"Logic and Metaphysics," "Ethics," "Moral Principles and Medical Practice" (for doctors).

CORNOLDI, J. M., S. J.—"The Physical System of St. Thomas."

CORTEZ—"Essays on Catholicity, Liberalism and Socialism."

DEVAS, C. S.—"The Key to the World's Progress."

DEVIVIER—"Christian Apologetics."

DE WULF-COFFEY—"Scholasticism Old and New."

DRISCOLL, J. T.—"Christian Philosophy," "God."

HETTINGER—"Natural Religion."

JOUIN, LOUIS, S. J.—"Logic and Metaphysics," "Moral Philosophy."

HILL, WALTER, S. J.—"Elements of Philosophy," "Moral Philosophy."

HOGAN, MICHAEL, S. J.—"Lord Bacon and Scholastic Philosophy."

HOLAIND, R. I., S. J.—"Natural Law and Legal Practice."

HUGHES, THOMAS, S. J.—"Anthropology and Biology."

HUMPHREY, S. J.—"Conscience and Law."

JOYCE, GEORGE H., S. J.—"Principles of Logic."

KLARMAN—"Crux of Pastoral Medicine" (for doctors).

KRESS—"Questions of Socialism and Their Answers."

LAMBERT, L. A.—"Christian Science Before the Bar of Reason."

LEO XIII.—"Great Encyclical Letters, with Preface by J. Wynne, S. J."

LEPICIER—"The Unseen World" (Spiritism).

LIBERATORE, MATTH., S. J.—"Political Economy."

MADDEN—"Reaction from Agnosticism."

MANNING, CARD.—"The Fourfold Sovereignty of God."

MERCIER, CARD.—"Relation of Experimental Psychology to Philosophy."

MING, JOHN J., S. J.—"Data of Modern Ethics," "Character and Religion of Modern Socialism."

MUCKERMAN, H., S. J.—"Attitude of Catholics Toward Darwinism," "The Humanizing of the Brute."

NEWMAN, CARD.—"An Essay Toward a Grammar of Assent."

POISSY, BRO. DE—"Elementary Course of Christian Philosophy."

POLAND, WM., S. J.—"The Laws of Thought," "The Truth of Thought," "Fundamental Ethics," "True Pedagogics and False Ethics."

RAUPERT—"Modern Spiritism," "The Danger of Spiritualism."

RICKABY, JOS., S. J.—"Political and Moral Essays."

RONAYNE, M., S. J.—"God Knowable and Known."

SCHWICKERATH, ROB., S. J.—"Jesuit Education."

SPALDING, RT. REV. J. L.—"Religion, Agnosticism and Evolution."

STANG, RT. REV.—"Socialism and Christianity."

STOECKL-FINLAY—"Handbook of the History of Philosophy."

THOMPSON, HANNA W. "The Brain and Personality."

TURNER, WM.—"History of Philosophy."

WALSH and O'MALLEY—"Pastoral Medicine" (for doctors).

WASMANN, ERIC, S. J.—"Instinct and Intelligence in the Animal Kingdom," "Modern Biology and Evolution," "Psychology of Ants and Higher Animals."

ALPHABETICAL INDEX.

Numbers, not pages, are referred to.

A BRIEF TEXT-BOOK OF

LOGIC AND MENTAL PHILOSOPHY

By REV. CHARLES COPPENS, S.J.

"The Stonyhurst Manuals gave decided proof that it was possible to make the study of logic, as well as metaphysics, popular and accessible to those who did not read the language of St. Thomas and the Schools. Nevertheless, the Stonyhurst Manuals were not text-books for the student. They helped him to an easier mastery of the practical value of the study in philosophy, but they were not digested for the study in school. Father Coppens has gone further. He has ventured to give us a school text which gathers into a small compass the concise definitions, principles, and rules found in standard class books, such as Liberatore, Zigliara, Van der Aa, and others of equal authority. . . . Father Coppens' book will be a safe, a very safe guide, and a very easy one, considering the subject-matter, for young students of philosophy. Their Latin text-books will be better understood and appreciated for this help, of which we urge everyone who may begin the study of philosophy to avail himself at once. Indeed, we have not the slightest misgiving that the small manual will prove a most valuable aid both to those who pursue the two years course, and much more to others who can devote only one year to it, or who, having failed in the thorough mastery of a system of philosophy heretofore, are anxious to supply the loss at the least possible cost of time and severe application."—*American Ecclesiastical Review.*

"Father Coppens, we think, has produced a book which will meet all the requirements of the English student of philosophy. It embodies a thorough course of Logic and Metaphysics, expressed in clear, concise language, and is printed with a care for those details— division of questions, diversity of type, accentuation of paragraphs, etc.—which go to make up a text-book, and cannot fail to arrest and fix the attention of the reader. Needless to say, the Encyclical of the Holy Father has been the inspiration of the learned author, and the philosophy of St. Thomas permeates the whole work. We feel assured it will meet with a hearty welcome in all our schools and colleges."—*Ave Maria.*

"I received from your publisher your admirable work on 'Logic and Mental Philosophy.' It is just the work needed at the present time, and I earnestly recommend its use in our colleges."—P. J. RYAN, Archbishop of Philadelphia.

"Your book on Logic and Metaphysics is an admirable textbook."—J. L. SPALDING, Bishop of Peoria.

A BRIEF TEXT-BOOK OF
MORAL PHILOSOPHY

By REV. CHARLES COPPENS, S.J.

"This volume may be described as a primer of the best kind. It covers the whole ground of doctrinal ethics. It is brief, while at the same time invariably clear. In statement it is exact without pedantry, in method it is scholastic, but neither tedious nor antiquated. Examples from daily life and topics of current discussion are everywhere introduced to give reality and animation to the treatment. . . . The secret of his success is to be found in his choice of materials and in their judicious employment. . . . To those who desire precise and intelligent statement of the doctrines held by all Catholic philosophers, on almost every point of moral philosophy, and in particular on those topics about which controversy is so earnest at the present moment, this little treatise will be very acceptable. A novel feature of the book is the terse manner in which objections are stated and dealt with."—*Dublin Review*.

"The excellent text-book of Father Coppens we esteem very highly and use very frequently in our literary work."—ARTHUR PREUSS.

THE ART OF ORATORICAL COMPOSITION

BASED ON THE PRECEPTS AND MODELS OF THE GREAT MASTERS

By REV. CHARLES COPPENS, S.J.

"It is a clear, didactic exposition, with such illustrations from modern sources as will make it practical under our circumstances. But it is also a text-book, which is saying something apart from its general merits, as teachers will understand. . . . Least of all has Father Coppens reason to guard himself against distrust, for he simply proves his strength by the grasp he has of the masters in his profession. . . . For seminaries, we find here the entire course from preparatory school to the class of sacred eloquence in theology."—*American Catholic Quarterly Review*.

"Father Coppens has been, over twenty-five years, a Professor of Oratory in the United States, so that he brings to this book not only the full equipment of a master of the art, but all the invaluable skill in imparting his knowledge to be acquired only, and after long trial, in the rostrum of the teacher. Father Coppens' is perhaps the most practical class book on the speaker's art yet offered to American schools. . . . Father Coppens, wherever it is practicable, lets the acknowledged masters of oratorical composition speak for themselves, so that his pupil is made familiar, and in their own words, with the leading precepts of the great writers on oratory among both the ancients and moderns."—*Catholic World*.

A PRACTICAL INTRODUCTION TO
ENGLISH RHETORIC
PRECEPTS AND EXERCISES
By REV. CHARLES COPPENS, S.J.

This work is modestly called by the author an 'Introduction,' but it is in reality a thorough treatise on rhetoric and poetry. As a text-book for Catholic colleges and academies, it has no rival in the English language. Its value, from a literary point of view, is of the highest order, and it is the only rhetoric published in the United States, in England, or in Ireland that even attempts to give an extensive criticism of standard literature from a Catholic standpoint.

Speaking of the "Rhetoric," Very Rev. Rudolph Meyer, S.J., said: "The best thing I ever did for education was to urge Father Coppens to publish that book."

"We have taken some of the most popular and approved text-books in use in our best schools and compared them with this new 'Introduction to English Rhetoric.' The result is in every way—and in some parts to an exceptional degree—favorable to the latter." —*American Catholic Quarterly Review.*

"We are happy to add another to the list of text-books for Catholic schools of which one can write only in terms of unqualified praise. Its author, the Rev. Charles Coppens, S.J., is already well known through his admirable 'Art of Oratorical Composition.' His two books, taken together, contain the entire course of rhetoric as studied in colleges and universities. But the 'Practical Introduction to English Rhetoric,' taken alone, must have a far wider sphere of usefulness, being perfectly adapted for the higher departments of academies for girls, and for the use of the teachers themselves in the lower departments of schools for either sex, or in schools where so extended a course of rhetoric does not enter into the plan of study."—*The Pilot.*